THE THINGS THEY DIDN'T TEACH YOU IN SEMINARY

Priceless Jewels for Practical
Church Leadership

Dr. Derrick J. Hughes

LIFE TO LEGACY

Cover design by: Legacy Design Inc
        Legacydesigninc@gmail.com

Published by
Life To Legacy, LLC
P.O. 1239
Matteson, IL 60443
877-267-7477
www.Life2Legacy.com
Life2legacybooks@att.net

TABLE OF CONTENTS

DEDICATION

It is with humble appreciation that I dedicate this book to my dad, Archie N. Hughes. He was a man who was limited in learning, but as I watched his life, he gave me priceless jewels to live by; for that, I am eternally grateful to have had, in my opinion, the best dad in history. Although he is now resting with the Lord, his impact on my life lives on.

FOREWORD

Early on in the pandemic, the former President of the United States stood before the American people to make a hard request. Trump announced the Coronavirus Task Force plan, "15 Days to Slow the Spread." Trump, in that moment, declared from his podium, something that would be hard for the church in America to swallow. Churches would need to ask their members not to come. Visitation of elderly members would need to cease. The normal operations of church life would have to alter.

In this moment, churches in America would have to recognize and begin to become acquainted with a reality that churches in Asia and Europe were already experiencing. A virus was, and is, still spreading throughout the world. Research says that it passes from one person to another just by inhaling and exhaling, something that is completely unavoidable. So, churches, havens of salvation, and hospitals for sinners, needed to close. For Christians were not immune to this insidious disease. Indeed, churches in South Korea were hot-spots for the outbreak of the disease. Churches needed to do what so many others in society had done; cease having corporate worship and change the way they did church.

Even with all of the changes, both globally and locally, the church is still the church. Jesus Christ is the same yesterday, today, and forever (Heb 13:8). He is still Lord whether we have gathered together on Sundays physically or not. The church, we have come to understand in concrete terms, is not a building. We are the body of Christ through our spiritual connection with God and with one another.

To attack the issue of disconnection, many churches have moved to an online platform. Many churches had already established the necessity of communicating with their congregants via the internet. But now, many churches, most of whom were completely unprepared, have been forced to establish virtual churches. For the protection of congregations, this format is the best way to maintain community.

This is the best way to continue support for ministry in a time when the church is nowhere on people's priority list. People are anxious about whether they will contract this terrible disease. The last thing on their minds is supporting the church. But, this is not to say the church is not on their minds. People, unlike many other times, are thirsting for the community and the salvation that the church offers. This thirst, however, does not always translate into financial support. In the midst of this crisis, the church stands to offer services even when there is not an exchange of support.

Whatever illusion many in the church had about its insulation from the surrounding world has been destroyed. Government policy, hospital guidelines, even to the transformation of social and cultural etiquette, has changed the way we do church. It has become popular as of late in black church spaces for people to tell others to touch others in affirmation of a sermonic point. That has all changed. Now, we are told, no one needs to touch anyone else for our own safety. Things have irrevocably changed, whether we want to accept it or not. The church exists in the real world. What happens in it affects the way we live out our vocation as church.

In this important book, *The Things They Didn't Teach You In Seminary: Priceless Jewels for Practical Church Leadership*, Dr. Derrick J. Hughes explores this very important theme: pastors should most certainly go to school. Seminary is an all-important and necessary institution that assures that ministers of the gospel are informed of church tradition and practice. To be the church, the church must be able to connect with ways that supports the church's effectiveness. Furthermore, to be an effective church, we must be willing to challenge the ways we have always conducted church. Theologians and biblical scholars have famously advanced the notion that we must always be willing to challenge the current church to ascertain if we have been faithful to the original tenets of the church's mission. This necessary challenge does not always occur in the context of church life without the prodding of the church's academic bodies.

But there are certain things, simply put, that Seminary cannot teach. Indeed, Seminary was not made to teach everything the minister of the gospel was supposed to know. Some things must be learned on the ground, in the fight. Previous historical examples can only teach so much. It is certainly of tremendous importance to know the parallels of *Enuma Elish* and Genesis. It is absolutely necessary for the minister polemical nature of the belief that Jesus was Son of God in a world where Caesar was also proclaimed as *divi filius*, God's son. But how one takes this enhanced knowledge of Genesis' connection to the Ancient Near Eastern world and the controversial nature of the church's proclamation of the gospel, is only learned in the practice of being a church in the world. Seminary cannot teach us everything we need to know to be the church.

In a time like no other, with unprecedented change and challenge to the traditional way of being the church, we need a guide like this that offers a heads up on the gaps in knowledge we may have. For those who have gone to Seminary and those who did not, the practice of ministry requires that someone inform us what it will take to be successful. Ministers do not always have this kind of counsel. They may not have mentors, fathers and mothers of the faith, who guide them in their journey towards ministry success. With such a gap in information, this book will be a blessing to those of us who need wisdom to guide out footsteps.

Dr. Derrick Hughes draws on his own personal triumphs and failures, in addition to his own training, to provide the reader with a bridge over the pitfalls of ministry. Anyone who has done ministry for a day will recognize that the vicissitudes of ministry will generate all sorts of low moments. Because of this, we need a helpful voice who will warn of the upcoming challenges that we might face. There are things in ministry that change constantly. We will not be able to predict all of them. But this book will open our eyes to the possible difficulties that may come so that, with God's help, we can maintain the victory and serve God's people effectively.

—Dr. Ralph Douglas West

INTRODUCTION

"It takes two tracks to carry the weight of a freight train. Similarly, doing ministry from a practical standpoint and an academic standpoint are two separate tracks. Experience is the tie that brings both tracks together to carry the weight of an effective and fulfilling ministry."

If there has ever been a time that a solid seminary education has been necessary to meet the challenges of people immersed in an information age, that time is now. More than ever, pastors must step up to the plate and be able to deliver substantive and relevant messages to congregants who can fact-check your sermon points while you are in the midst of preaching your sermon. Most notably, access to information has simultaneously enhanced and complicated a pastor's role. Not only from a homiletic point of view must his message delivery be spot on, but his teaching and sermons must include the material that will hold the attention of a generation that thrives on instant content that's governed by a short attention span. Therefore, the benefits of attending a good seminary helps establish a solid foundation on which an effective, thriving ministry can be built.

Academic curriculums that are strong in church history help stave off heresies that reemerge in modern times. Being skilled in how to exegete a text in the original languages and how to prepare an expository message with impactful application points are critical. The skill to make historical narratives and foundational Christianity adaptable and relevant to today's congregants without veering off doctrinal course is essential. These and many other skill sets must be developed after one matriculates and moves on to master the skill sets learned during postgraduate studies.

Whereas being strong academically is essential, it is also a trap into which many ministers and pastors fall. Whereas people love useful information, the dissemination of information addresses only a small portion of the complex dynamic that congregants bring to church. One soon finds that it's not the theological information that must be mastered, it's the people's information. You have to know and to lead people within the context of their reality. Knowing church history is not going to help you with understanding their history. How to meet people's physical, emotional, social and spiritual needs often has to be addressed before the benefit of theological information can be of use. People won't be interested in the significance of the Protestant Reformation when their reformation is at stake. You have discerned what the correct approach is to lead God's people. Problems don't simply go away with a pithy catchphrase or a Bible verse. Often you have to labor and travail with people through their issues. Only then will people reach the "buy-in" point once they see that the pastor and the church are concerned about their needs. Jesus not only preached to the five thousand, but he didn't want to send them away hungry, so he fed them too. True ministry addresses the needs of both the spiritual and the natural man within the context of a healthy congregational environment.

Learning about ministry and learning how to do effective ministry are two different things. Using the wrong strategies can be detrimental. For example, in the medical field, treating the wrong ailment can have devastating results. An incorrect diagnosis means the wrong intervention. The wrong intervention means the real problem goes untreated, which can ultimately result in death. Therefore, the pastor's role requires wisdom and the sagacity of being able to hear from God and understand all of the issues people bring to the table. But it's not just the personal issues that must be worked through. The organizational, congregational, social, political, financial and all of the other problems must be managed as well. The wrong diagnosis leads to the wrong intervention, which can contribute to the death of a ministry.

Cerebral knowledge is good. What books teach is great. That's what seminary supplies. However, which seminary course or courses are going to make you proficient in all the areas of pastoral ministry necessary to lead a 21st century thriving church? For example, how do you handle the influential congregate who opposes the pastor's vision for the church? Is there a course for that? No. This is where the downfall lies. This is the dilemma that many seminary graduates will face once they walk across the stage to receive their degree and head to the local church down the street. There are some things that only experience can teach you—not a curriculum, not a textbook.

This book is for those who want to avoid some of the pitfalls one will inevitably encounter between the journey from the commencement ceremony to the congregation. While this writer emphasizes the necessity of obtaining a good seminary education, I also want to dispel the myth that a seminary degree prepares you for what you will encounter in a real-world church; it doesn't. Through my many ups and downs, successes and failures, I will share with you many impactful lessons and experiences that will serve as a bridge over the troubled waters of real-life ministry that have dimmed the hopes of many bright-eyed seminary graduates.

However, my experience bases are not founded upon my career as a minister and pastor only, but I also bring considerable academic credentials. I have an earned Doctor of Ministry Degree from United Theological Seminary in Dayton, Ohio, a Master of Arts Degree in Urban Ministry with Cum Laude honors from Trinity Evangelical Divinity School in Deerfield, Illinois, and a Bachelor of Science Degree in Business Administration from Xavier University in Cincinnati, Ohio.

In addition to my classroom accomplishments as a student, I have taught at both the undergraduate and graduate levels as an adjunct professor at Trinity Evangelical Divinity School and Trinity International University of Deerfield, Illinois. I have instructed students on subjects ranging from Urban Ministry Practicum, Argumentation and Persuasive Speaking, Foundations of Christian Counseling, Urban Sociology, The Sociological Aspects of the Book of Acts, American Government, Christian Thinking and Living, Practical Theology, Discipleship Across the Life Span and Life Assessment.

With decades of ministerial experience and academic achievement, I have been tried and tested. Therefore, it is my sincerest aspiration that my experience and knowledge can be of significant benefit as I share with you my priceless jewels for practical church leadership.

Chapter 1

The Success and Failures of Seminary

In a technology-driven world, every segment of society, whether it be positive or negative, has been significantly impacted. How we communicate, socialize, engage politically and particularly how we learn is evolving at a rapid pace. Therefore, in order to keep pace with a shifting socioeconomic, geopolitical, multicultural landscape, every organization and institution is forced to adapt or fall behind the times and become ineffective. The same is true for today's seminaries and their approach to addressing the rapid shifts in cultural norms. Herein is the challenge for today's theological institutions. How to stay relevant in offering coursework and experiential opportunities that actually prepare seminarians to be effective leaders, while staying grounded in solid, biblically based education is challenging. However, since not all cultural change is good, seminaries must guard against drifting away from the fundamentals of Christian faith as societal norms shift deeper into secularism.

The success and failure of seminaries can be measured in many ways. According to a Seminary Comparison chart published by Dallas Theological Seminary[1] (DTS), enrollment trends are informative. From the years 2009 through 2017, there were no drastic declines in enrollment at thirty-six of the top seminaries, but by 2017 enrollment numbers started trending downward. In 2009, Fuller Seminary led the way with over 4,000 enrollees, while distant seconds were DTS (2,102), Southern Baptist Theological Seminary (SBTS) with 2,585, Trinity Evangelical Divinity School (TEDS) with 1,407 and Reformed Theological Seminary (RTS) with 1,140. Fast-forward to 2017, and Fuller's numbers were down to 2,897, a 28% decrease. DTS was up 18% to 2,369, SBTS was up 5% to 2719, TEDS enrollment numbers were down 22% to 1,101 and RTS down 7%. Out of the thirty-six schools surveyed, increased, and decreased enrollment numbers split 50/50.

Of the five schools identified above, the stats for hours per curriculum for Bible, Theology, Languages and Electives are as follows: Fuller, Bible and theology outpaced languages and electives. DTS, languages outpaced the other categories, with theology and electives second, and Bible last. At SBTS, electives were first, Bible and theology second, and languages last. At TEDS, electives held a narrow margin over the other three categories, which held equal ranking. Finally, at RTS, theology led the way, Bible was second, languages third, and electives last.

Why are the stats on coursework important? According to the InTrust report[2], the number of students enrolling in the M. Div. Programs (the degree required for ordination in many organizational churches) has been on the decline for years. Some contributing factors to this decline are that there are more churches that do not require a seminary degree for ordination. Secondly, the expense of obtaining the degree leaves many graduates strapped in debt, and they cannot afford to accept jobs at churches that would underpay them. Therefore, some churches are not recruiting full-time pastors because they cannot afford to pay a compensable and competitive salary and provide benefits.

Clearly, there are some valleys to overcome, yet seminaries are still attracting students who wish to further their careers in ministry. Fluctuations in enrollment numbers are expected. However, when there are so many attractive career choices available, the fact that there are students interested in entering seminary itself is a positive sign. Honestly, things could be better. The losses do not overwhelm the gains. Indeed, there are some bright spots. For example, minority and women enrollment numbers are on the rise. Another interesting trend is that the number of churches that do not require a seminary education is increasing. Many of these churches are nondenominational, independent, Pentecostal and charismatic. In such cases, ministers who are not seeking an advanced degree might still attend seminary to focus on a specific area of learning that better prepares them for ministry. Many seminaries offer Certificate Programs that are for those who have already obtained a degree from a secular school, but want to further their education by being trained in specific areas to enhance their ministerial career. These programs offer an array of introductory courses and provide a good foundation so that a minister can have some basic educational tools and resources needed to be more effective in church leadership.

Many seminaries also partner with churches in the surrounding communities to offer extension courses that students can attend within the familiarity of their home church. Programs such as these bring the school to the student and alleviate the barrier of "going to school." To even further scale the barrier of the classroom setting, a significant percentage of students are now enrolling in online courses. In this category, many of the top-tier seminaries offer an array of courses that attract those who have careers or domestic challenges and cannot enroll in a traditional classroom setting. Some degrees can be earned online using interactive technology to educate students from the comfort of their home.

All these educational modalities and programs offered by seminaries are positives that are in keeping with what the Bible encourages: "Study to shew thyself approved unto God, a workman that needeth not to be ashamed, rightly dividing the word of truth" (2 Timothy 2:15, KJV). When it comes to serving an omniscient, omnipotent and omnipresent God in the context of the home, church or community, we should want only to offer Him and those we serve our very best. We should aspire to the highest level of attainable education so that we will be trained to face the rigors of an oppositional secular world and be equipped to meet the needs of a demanding congregation.

EXCEPTIONS TO THE RULE

Considering all of the issues a pastor must face leading a flock of God's people, I believe that ministers should be held to the same educational and ethical standards that we do with other professions such as doctors, dentists, lawyers and teachers. On the other hand, some are of the opinion that ministers should not be viewed as other professionals, but as more of a calling that cannot be initiated by institutional education. However, no matter what side of the debate that you fall on, one question remains. Is it necessary that you obtain a seminary degree in order to be effective in ministry? The answer, absolutely not. Historically, not everyone has been able to obtain an undergraduate degree, let alone attend a seminary. Yet there are thousands of thriving churches all over the United States and throughout the world where there is non-seminarian leadership in place and the churches are flourishing.

One well-known pastor of historical significance who made a huge impact on evangelical Christianity in the United States was Dwight L. Moody, founder of Moody Memorial Church in Chicago and the Moody Bible Institute. According to an online article published by *Christianity Today*, Moody had the equivalent of a fifth-grade education.[3] He was a masterful and powerful evangelist who realized the importance of establishing institutions to train individuals for the work of the ministry, though he had no formal training. His powerful revivals and crusades drew countless thousands of souls to Christ and were popular because he included a music ministry, recruiting famed gospel singers. What Moody lacked in education, God compensated for in the demonstration of power. To this day, Moody's name is synonymous with excellence throughout the world through Moody Memorial Church, its seminary, Moody Bible Institute, broadcast network (WMBI), publishing company (Moody Press) and other ministry-related entities—all started by an anointed preacher with a fifth-grade education.

Another example of a very successful pastor of a cutting-edge church who is not a graduate of a seminary is H.B. Charles Jr., pastor of

Shiloh Metropolitan Baptist Church in Jacksonville, Florida. Charles is the perfect, albeit rare, example of a thriving pastoral career without the academic credentials but who is also respected among accomplished scholars. As a dynamic preacher who regularly speaks on platforms typically reserved for seminarians and scholars, Charles is known for his brilliant sermonic content and polished homiletic style. He has attracted the attention of scholars through the United States for years now and was recently conferred an honorary Doctorate of Divinity at Master's Theology Seminary by Dr. John MacArthur. The honorary doctorate degree is conferred by a seminary on rare occasions to individuals who have accomplished great things in ministry and is used by God in doing kingdom work in remarkable ways. When someone with the status of John MacArthur confers an honorary on someone, it is noteworthy. In regards to his invitations to speak in prestigious venues, H.B. Charles has preached in many, including at the Ligonier Ministries Conferences founded by the late, great Dr. R.C. Sproul, where he stands in company with other great internationally celebrated scholars as John MacArthur, James Montgomery Boice and many others.

Though there are other examples that we could cite, these two highly regarded individuals are noteworthy examples of the doors God can open without the aid of seminary education. However, the key factor in both of their successes—experience played the primary role.

THE OBJECTIONS TO SEMINARY TRAINING

There are many benefits to attending seminary, such as providing structured and systematic training in an array of theological, biblical, ethical, ecclesiastical and administrative subjects that is more effective in a classroom setting. There is also the accountability of being under a pedagogical system where performance is evaluated and where grades count. The relationships and friendships with fellow classmates and staff are fulfilling and, in some cases, lifelong. Though challenging, and sometimes downright stressful, the upside is that a good seminary training can open career doors and opportunities that would not be available otherwise.

So why wouldn't a person want to attend seminary? Besides being too expensive, too long, requiring too many unnecessary classes, not being culturally or contextually sensitive and inclusive, not keeping up with the times and many other objections, there are some understandable reasons why some opt out of seminary. Listed below are four reasons why ministers do not attend seminary.

1) In many churches, there is no requirement to have a seminary degree in order to become the pastor. This is particularly true in non-denominational and independent churches, where faithfulness to the ministry, tenure, preaching, teaching and leadership skills, the ability to connect with and having the respect of the congregants, and character are the deciding factors.

2) The average minister may not have a bachelor's level of education. Seminary is a postgraduate program. Many pastors who have been out of school for decades simply wouldn't qualify or be able to keep up academically.

3) Another barrier for some is that if you are already a senior pastor and/or pastoring full-time, you already have a wealth of wisdom and experience. Ministers at this level of ministry simply do not have the time to fit in a course load of academic studies with their current responsibilities of running a church. The theory and practicums one engages in at seminary are roads they have already traveled experientially and would amount to retracing ground they have already covered.

4) Another issue is that seminary can challenge the religious traditions and beliefs that a person may hold. Depending upon the seminary you attend, liberal or conservative, protestant or Catholic, you could walk away conflicted and confused. Some people are simply afraid to have their belief systems challenged or destroyed.

For example, a person who was raised in a Pentecostal church but attending an evangelical school might be confronted with a curriculum that teaches spiritual gifts went out with the closing of the canon of Scriptures, and women shouldn't be pastors. However, this person has a female pastor and believes in operating in spiritual gifts. These are two conflicting doctrinal positions. If the seminaries in this person's area are all evangelical, maybe this individual would think twice about attending one of those schools.

The fact is that there are pros and cons on both sides of the debate about attending seminary. In this aspect of my study, the point has not been to take sides, but to examine different viewpoints. However, the following chapters shall be dedicated to the main premise of this book, which is that no matter how great of a formal education you receive, the classroom does not fully prepare you for the day-to-day life in the church.

Things the Classroom Can't Teach

If you ask the average graduate of seminary if they are ready for the trials of ministry, they would respond with a resounding yes. They've studied, they've researched, and they've written themselves all the way to earning a degree. For all practical purposes, they have arrived. Right? Then it's time to find a church home. They successfully searched for a church, went through the selection process, interviewed for a pastoral or ministry staff position, and they got the job. All these successes add more notches to their proverbial gun. Now they are ready to take on the world. But that's the irony concerning the path they have been traveling thus far. It's not the world outside the church that they really have to take on. It's the world inside the church that they will have to confront. The problem is, at this point they don't know what it is that they don't know. They are indeed the new kid on the block. The only difference is that they are in the leadership role.

The reality is that they soon find out that they are expected to know how to manage that for which they have not been prepared, in a critical space that does not lend itself to on-the-job training and rookie mistakes. When you take over a church, you hit the ground running. Depending on the condition of the church, which you only find out after you take the job, you have no idea what you are really walking into.

You soon find out that congregational conflagrations get awfully hot, and spread quickly. In the heat of a congregational crisis is a bad time to find out that a pastor has to be a skilled firefighter. How to fight fires is critically important. You cannot respond to a grease fire with water, because you'll only make matters worse.

Some of the most trying times a pastor can face are church fights, such as senior staff vying for power, a major congregational power player galvanizing a faction to defy or change church policy, or you have an Absalom on your hands and a significant portion of the church wants to follow him, thus yielding to church splits. And of course, a new pastor can walk into a financial crisis caused by mismanagement of church funds by previous leadership.

These are just a few scenarios that a new pastor can face taking over a new church. Though the new pastor needs a job, they also need to ask the right questions before taking the reins of leadership. In the coming chapters, we will address other critical circumstances to avoid in order to maintain a healthy church.

CRASH AND BURN

There are some things from which a seminary degree cannot insulate you. The main one is yourself. That's right. Despite all of the external pressures that could take down a pastor, the one pitfall that must be avoided is being your own worst enemy. As the old saying goes, "You're never too old to learn." Let's piggyback on that and add, you're never too mighty to crash and burn, either.

There are many reasons crashing and burning are possibilities that could destroy a church or a ministry. The main one is pride. As the Bible teaches in Proverbs, "Pride *goeth* before destruction, and a haughty spirit before a fall" (Proverbs 16:18, KJV). Some of the most seductive influences that can tempt a minister are influence and authority. Respect is hard to gain but very easy to lose. A congregation's willingness to follow you has to be treated with the utmost respect. However, pride makes you think you can cross the line and still be in the safe zone— but the truth is that you are headed for a crash and burn. When you violate Christian behavior as a leader, you are making a mockery out of the program of God. God has put you in position to show people how to speak, live, and think. It is your responsibility to lead, to be an example to the flock (1 Peter 5:3). More than anything you must be a better Christian than you are a preacher/pastor/church leader. God expects you to consecrate Him before the people (Num. 20:12). People ought to be able to examine your entire life and see and hear you representing Jesus. Your earthly assignment is to make God look so wonderful that your reflection of Him entices people to want Him as you do.

As a church leader, you ought to be so much in love with God that your life exudes your love for God so much so, that it says, watch my love for God and follow me. It should not just be seen in how you do ministry (preach/teach and administrate), but how you love the Holy One. Though there are many cases where a pastor gets fired or forced to resign amidst scandal or because of some immoral action, a couple of recent cases that also made headlines come to mind. The first is Bill Hybels, former pastor of Willow Creek Community Church in South Barrington, Illinois, had to resign amidst several credible allegations of sexual misconduct. Hybels pastored one of the largest evangelical churches in America, with a regular attendance of over 20,000, on their sprawling campus in Barrington. He was a celebrated author, and through his Willow Creek Association and Global Leadership Summit, linked thousands of churches and trained thousands of pastors and ministers in the principles of church leadership. Though God is forgiving, and we must pray for those who have fallen, in many cases the damage caused in the wake of some such improprieties is irreparable. However, the ones most hurt are countless individuals whose faith in the church has been damaged due to the misconduct of a trusted leader. Though there is still controversy surrounding the validity of all the allegations against Hybels, some of which he was proven innocent, this still serves as an object lesson as to how you can still crash and burn after reaching the pinnacle of success.

Lastly, we were all shocked when allegations surfaced concerning the late Ravi Zacharias, one of the most influential Christian apologists of our time who apparently was steeped in sexual sin and abusing women for years. Though he was not a pastor, he was a renowned church leader with enormous international influence. Once the scandal broke, instead of being contrite and repenting, he maintained his innocence, and vigorously fought to discredit his accusers. After an independent investigation was completed RZIM (Ravi Zacharias International Ministries) stated that the allegations were credible, and that they are renaming the ministry and removing his content.[4] After the voluminous apologetic work he produced over decades of ministry, the last chapter of his life's story is disgraceful leaving his family, his ministry, all those who believed in him and the ones he abused to bear the indignity and impact of his actions.

Though there are numerous reasons why church leaders can fail, there are two truths that I will cover later in this book that everyone in church leadership should heed: (1) These are not your people, and (2) it's God's church, not yours. In order to realize the success and avoid the failure, lead God's people and manage God's church with the heart of a lion and the humility of a servant, walking faithfully in the fulfillment of your calling, all to God's glory—not yours.

CHAPTER 2

SERVING IN THE RIGHT PLACE

It was once asked, why would anyone in their right mind want to be a pastor? When you consider all of what a spiritual leader must go through to lead a group of people who are often obstinate, rebellious, self-centered, self-willed, despise correction but like sheep need a shepherd, but don't really want one, it makes sense to ask, why would someone want to put themselves through that?

Think of all the issues a pastor must deal with that he can't unknow. All the nitty-gritty, nasty stuff that is brought to him in confidence; about individuals, marriages and families that must be kept confidential, not even sharing with a spouse, yet staying humble, impartial, nonjudgmental, and loving, without violating legal, ethical, or biblical standards. It's a very tight rope to walk.

But that's not all. Since pastors are teachers, they also incur a stricter judgment (James 3:1). They have to watch out for the congregation and give account to God for those souls (Heb. 13:17). Giving an account for your own soul is a big enough task by itself, let alone being accountable to God for someone else's soul. So, before some starry-eyed seminary graduate says, "Here I am Lord, send me," you better also consider what Jesus asked Peter three times: "Do you love me?" Each time Peter said, "Yes, Lord, you know I do." The Lord's response was, "Feed my sheep." Pastoring God's people must be based on a love for the Lord, and a desire to feed (care for) God's sheep under circumstances that will try your soul.

When you are in love, oftentimes you're not in your "right mind." In many cases, you ignore what is obvious but are driven by passion to please the one whom you love. Like the '70s song "Walking in the Rain With the One You Love" that encapsulates the actions of two people in love oblivious to the nuisance of getting wet while walking in the rain. However, tamp down that passion some, and it becomes a new song, "Let's Walk After the Rain Is Over." Love allows you to continue when you would normally give up.

Dealing with people in ministry from the basis of your natural mind, your response is different. You might start thinking and saying the wrong thing. After being pointed out in a crowd, Peter started cursing. The counterbalance is the love of Christ that constrains us. And the power of God that keeps us. In your right mind (your natural mind), you cannot pastor God's people. It must be, "not by power, nor by might, but by God's spirit and faith that works by love."

At some point, every congregation will need a new pastor. Whether the former pastor has resigned, retired, expired, or was fired, recruiting the right leadership can be quite an undertaking. Though the average tenure of a pastor may be five to seven years or some much longer, at some point the church will need to make a change in leadership. On the flip side of the coin, there will be some potential pastoral candidate who responds to the call hoping to come in and take the church to the next level. This sets up an interesting dynamic for both the church and the candidate, because they may have unrealistic expectations of each other. You can only have a win-win situation when the right pastor comes to the right church.

NAVIGATING THE SEARCH

I have been in pastoral leadership nearly three decades. I have been at the helm of ministry leadership for multiple size churches. I have led a church plant, a small congregation, a medium size, and two large congregations of several thousands, one where I was on staff and the other one I currently lead as senior pastor. Of those four churches that I was the pastor, I have been called to three and planted one. It has been my esteemed honor to be a pastor. Of all the experiences of being a pastor, I must say that receiving the actual calls from three of the churches were certainly some of the most exhilarating moments in ministry for me. To hear that a group of people have decided that you are the person who they want to lead them spiritually is beyond words. As a result of experiencing the candidating process, I hope that what I have to offer will be a benefit to you.

Some of the characteristics that a church looks for in its search for a new pastor is his skill set, academics, prior assignments, credentials, endorsements, etc. Obviously, the candidate pastor will have to have a sterling reputation and meet the biblical standards of morality. Another characteristic that could have a bearing on whether a pastor is considered for hire is his marital status. Most congregations would probably be more comfortable with a married pastor, because it is an indicator of stability in his personal life. How well a pastor treats his wife and manages his family says a lot about who he is away from the congregation. The Bible asks this question: how can a minister manage the church if he cannot manage his own family?

With these and other characteristics in mind, the hiring(pulpit) committee can size up a potential minister rather quickly. However, the biggest determining factor—which might be the simplest but most subjective reason—is whether they like him or not. Credentials and all the rest are fine, but the people have to like the candidate if they are going to offer the person the job. No matter what, people are people, and when it comes down to it, if they don't like you, in the long run, how well you teach or preach won't make much of a difference.

PERSONALITY PLAYS A PART

There are two forces that must connect in order for the pastor-and-church relationship to work. The personality of the pastor must match the personality of the people of the church. Most churches and pastoral candidates miss this concept. When I say "match" I mean in a complementary fashion. Both the potential pastor and the congregation must have a philosophical and ideological connection to forge a congenial relationship. Without a personality complement a strained relationship is inevitable. For example, in marriage, more arguments and conflicts leading to serious marital problems develop when one spouse is trying to change the other. Often the contentions are rooted in personality traits. Whereas adjustments can be made to accommodate differences, you're not going to change a person's personality.

According to *Merriam-Webster's Dictionary*, one of the definitions of personality is the *complex of characteristics that distinguishes an individual or a nation or group*. The aspect of this definition that is noteworthy is the *complex of characteristics*. What specifically is meant by complex? Let's turn once again to the dictionary: "complex" is defined as a *group of culture traits relating to a single activity*; in this case, the *cultural traits* and *single activity* would be associated with a particular church. Therefore, when applying the meaning of personality as related to a church, we understand that churches have personality traits.

We actually have a great example of church characteristics or personality being identified and evaluated in the Book of Revelation, where the Lord commends, corrects and encourages the seven churches of Asia Minor. At each church, the Lord identifies certain congregational traits that are either commendable or require correction, thus giving us a snapshot of that church's personality.

Therefore, in any church situation, the personality and culture of the people in the church must match the personality of the pastor. If they do not, you have a formula for disruption and, in extreme cases, disaster. For example, a pastor who is regimented and emphasizes tight structure trying to pastor a congregation that opposes regimentation could find himself in an irreconcilable situation. Under those circumstances, something will have to give. More than likely it will be the pastor.

I have served at churches whose relationship with their pastors had been challenging. A challenging relationship between pastor and people will create a robust culture that is not conducive for spiritual unity. It produces bad blood between all parties involved. Unfortunately, a bad relationship with one invites one to be suspect of having an ideal relationship with the next person or group. It leaves the church and the pastor blaming each other for the bad relationship when the real problem was they never should have married. The onus is on both parties to have the acumen to match the relationship before the marriage. Simply, every church regardless of the budget or size is not for every preacher and the skill set of the preacher is not for every church. You must agree (Amos 3:3).

A NEWER MODEL OF THE SAME CAR

What is a congregation really looking for in a new pastor? Of course, they want the minister to come in and do all of the primary duties of a pastor such as teach, preach, marry and bury. They want the pastor to do all the wonderful things like take the church to the next level, ushering in growth, expansion, and increase. They want to see the manifestation of the Lord's blessing poured out so that the people of the Lord can experience the abundant life of the child of God—with one small distinction. They do not really want to change anything. What they really want is a newer model of the same car. Don't switch models; just upgrade the one we have.

Change does not come naturally or easily. Many people live by the saying, "If it ain't broke, then don't fix it." Maintaining the status quo is comfortable. It's typical and familiar, and therefore more desirable. Whereas the new pastor—having big dreams, seeing new horizons and a brighter tomorrow—wants to enact a fresh vision for the church, the congregants are looking to keep things the same and are not interested in switching the model of their proverbial car.

Therefore, it is imperative that the pastor has a good grasp of the context of the church. What situations and circumstances have the church just come out of? What are the historic issues that have hindered the growth of the church? What is the personality of the church? How realistic for this congregation are the changes the pastor wants to make? Is it for the good of the people or is it for the pastor's good? How are decisions made? Who are the power players, and what makes them tick? These are the important questions that must be answered before a pastor embarks on pursuing a new vision. If these questions are not answered, the pastor may be leading a reluctant church down the wrong road filled with obstructions, potholes, and detours. Before you take up the pastor's mantle, determine first if serving there is the right place. Lastly, no matter what model the proverbial car is, if it's sitting on four flats, it's not going anywhere.

CHAPTER 3

BE SELFISH

Not long ago, I had to fly out of town for a speaking engagement. Once I boarded the plane and found my seat, I placed my carry-on bag in the overhead storage, sat down and strapped myself into the seat. Shortly after everyone was seated and the plane began backing away from the gate, the flight attendants took their places in the center cabin aisle and began giving their routine safety instructions. It was all very typical, predictable, something that anyone who has flown has heard a thousand times. However, this time was different.

When the flight attendant reached the portion of the instruction where they talk about what to do in case of a sudden loss of cabin pressure, something jumped out at me. They said, "If you are traveling with a small child or another that needs assistance, place your breathing mask on first, then help the other." Though I have heard this instruction countless times, it struck me that in some situations, you have to help yourself first before you can be of help to others. Musing further upon this, I thought, *the airlines got this one right*. It's more important for the adult to make sure they can breathe so they are able to help someone else in need. It does no one any good if the one who should be helping suffocates. This illustration helps emphasize that pastors cannot serve others without first taking care of themselves.

For purposes of clarification, there's a big difference between what

I mean by *be selfish* and the behavioral characteristics of *selfishness*. Webster's Dictionary defines *selfishness* as *a concern for one's own welfare or advantage at the expense of or in disregard of others: an excessive interest in oneself.* This definition represents the negative aspect of the word, because selfishness is exercised *at the expense of or in disregard of others.* However, what I am emphasizing here is the exact opposite of that definition. I am emphasizing being selfish *on the behalf of* and *for the betterment* of others. In other words, in order for a pastor to be effective in leadership, he must take care of himself first.

In 1 Corinthians, Paul makes an interesting statement:

> Do you not know that in a race all the runners run, but only one receives the prize? So run that you may obtain it. Every athlete exercises self-control in all things. They do it to receive a perishable wreath, but we an imperishable. So I do not run aimlessly; I do not box as one beating the air. But I discipline my body and keep it under control, lest after preaching to others I myself should be disqualified.
>
> 1 Corinthians 9:24-27

Here, Paul emphasizes the need for self-control. Why? Because he does not want to be a loser, after having run the race and after preaching to others, to end up being disqualified. Though it is debatable as to what *disqualified* actually means, whatever it is—it's not good. It's counter-productive, and it causes you to be a loser. Whether it's loss of reward or salvific in nature, it's bad. However, let me be clear that selfishness should not only be thought of in the context of something nefarious. Yes, the pastor must avoid things of a sinful nature, but he must also be aware of his limitations and abilities. Pastors are not superhuman. As James states in his epistle, we are men of "like passions" (James 5:17). We are only human, subject to error and mistakes. But being in leadership only exacerbates our mistakes, because the spotlight is on us, and others are depending on us for counsel and guidance. Therefore, like a well-oiled machine, we must be tuned up mentally, physically and spiritually in these critical areas so easily neglected in pastoral leadership.

In the Introduction, I discussed a few cases of crash and burn, where two very successful pastors ended up being fired or forced to resign because of some unfortunate indiscretion. In both cases, pride was the contributing factor that precipitated their fall. One of the effects of pride is that it insulates you from the Holy Spirit's conviction. Without being sensitive to the Spirit, you can minimize and in some cases even justify sin. You can reason with yourself that God doesn't mind. A little nibble here, a few dabbles there: I'm still all good with God. Right? Wrong!

BE TRUE TO YOURSELF

Years ago, there was a popular song titled "Be for Real." You have to know yourself and not let others put things on you that are not for you, or that you are not ready for. You must understand your frailties, proclivities, strengths, and weaknesses. You can only be who you are. A pastor is only as good as he is. But not as good as someone else wants him to be. If I try to be that who I am not, a fall is waiting at my doorstep. Here is where so many pastors have opened the door to pride and compromise: by trying to be someone who they are not. No one can be all things to all people. Not even the Lord would allow people to force Him into a position that was not a part of His mission. The people would have taken the Lord and made Him a king by force, but He withdrew Himself from them (see John 6:15).

FEED FROM YOUR SAUCER, NOT THE CUP

There was an old, wise preacher who once said, "When it comes to feeding God's people, make sure you feed from the saucer, not the cup." This statement is syntactically simple but philosophically profound. The cup represents what is contained in the preacher. What is contained in him is a result of his own time and investment in relation to the Lord. The quality of any relationship can be determined by the amount of time you spend with the other person, in this case, time with the Lord. However, I'm not talking about time spent in sermon or Bible study prep. No, I'm talking about quality time alone with God in prayer and meditation. Not for the congregation's sake, but for yours. This then is your cup. A life of daily devotion is of the utmost importance. The preacher who fails in devotion will ultimately fail in the ministry. Get the preacher ready, then allow God to get the sermon ready.

I cannot stress enough the importance of your daily time with God. Being in His presence is your power source. You are not ready to do ministry that day without first spending quality time with God. Will you feel any different? Probably not. You do just as Sampson did, engage in battle without realizing his strength was gone. Herein is the problem: our spiritual weakness is covered up by our human ability to do ministry.

It was Manuel Scott Sr. who said, "The better the persons are at preaching sermons are often the ones who are not good at living sermons." Why? We know how to do ministry. We've done it before. We know how to prepare a sermon, counsel, plan, and administrate. However, the real power of preparing sermons, counseling, planning, and administrating only comes from God. It is an insult to God to do His work without first seeking His presence in our lives. We need Him daily.

When you spend time with the Lord, He will fill your cup. What is in your cup is for you, so you can fulfill the calling where God has placed you. Once again, the Lord told Peter, "If you love me"—meaning having a relationship with me will enable you and put you in the position to—"feed my sheep." You cannot feed from an empty cup. Your cup has to be full and overflowing. It's overflow that runs down to the saucer where the sheep may feed. Again, in order for the sheep to feed from the saucer, you have to fill your cup until it is overflowing.

Jesus declared, "I am the vine, you are the branches...without me, you can do nothing" (John 15:5). Being a pastor does not insulate you from falling, but it could set the context for why you fall. Serving as a leader over people who trust you, hang on your every word, admire your gifts and want to follow you is too enticing for a pastor walking in his flesh. You must yield to the power and authority of the Lord. Too many people rely on their gifts that will not prevent a fall. You must take care of yourself first. Then you can take care of others. It is vitally important that you be selfish. Take care of your spiritual and natural nourishment first.

ANSWER THESE QUESTIONS:

1. How often do you pray?

2. How long do you pray? Jesus was disappointed that His disciples couldn't pray an hour with Him in a critical time of need. When is the last time you prayed at least an hour?

3. Do you have morning devotion with the Lord before you start your day?

4. Do you only read your Bible for sermon and study prep, or do you read it for joy of the Word and for cleansing?

5. If you are married, do you pray with your spouse?

6. How much secular television, movies, internet, social media are you watching? Are you investing the same amount or more time in spiritual enrichment?

7. When was the last time you got on your face and repented before the Lord, asking for his strength and mercy?

8. Giving is an act of worship and an indicator of what's really important to you. How much do you give back to the Lord?

Chapter 4

Be Clear About Your Purpose

When I first came to my current church in Florida, a pastor friend of mine in Memphis, the same place I pastored in before I left for Florida, called me to come and preach at his church. Of course, I gladly accepted the invitation. Right before I was to deliver my message that Friday evening, as was customary, the pastor gave the congregation some biographical information about me. It was all fine until he made a comment, which I am sure he meant as a compliment, but it struck me the wrong way and required some clarification. The pastor said that I had been "elevated to a new position." What he was implying was that I had left a *smaller* church to pastor a *larger* church, thereby being elevated. That didn't sit well with me.

Not only were there people in the congregation from my former church there to support me, but I did not want his implicit characterization and comparison of the lesser to greater to strike them the wrong way, either.

As soon as I stepped up to the pulpit, I thanked him for his gracious introduction and expressed my gratitude for being invited, but I then made it clear that it was just as great of an honor to serve at my former church as it was to serve at my current church. It has nothing to do with prestige or numbers, because the fact is, I do not deserve to be anyone's pastor. It was by grace and grace alone. I serve as a pastor at the pleasure and grace of God. No matter where I am called to pastor, large or small, I have been called to be a servant, not to glory in the assignment. This is why knowing your purpose is so important. In 2 Corinthians chapter 4, where Paul disavows deceit in his preaching, he makes these comments: "For what we preach is not ourselves, but Jesus Christ as Lord, and ourselves as your servants for Jesus' sake… But we have this treasure in jars of clay to show that this all-surpassing power is from God and not from us" (2 Corinthians 4:5,7, NIV). Paul has it right. It is not about us, but rather about the church of God and the furtherance of the Gospel. The excellence is of Him. As the King James version of this passage translates it, we are merely "earthen vessels." Only when you know *whose you are* can you better understand *who you are*, and from that vantage point alone can you understand your purpose.

THE PITFALLS OF DISTRACTION

On your journey as a pastor it is easy to get caught up in all the distractions along the way. It's easy to get caught up in the numbers game. No matter whether the numbers concern how many members or how much money, the temptation to keep up with the Joneses will take you off course. Once you fall victim to the pitfalls of distraction, you lose sight of your purpose, then you will be driven by the pursuit of wrong motives.

When the Pharisees came to John the Baptist, they made this comment:

> And they came to John and said to him, "Rabbi, he who was with you across the Jordan, to whom you bore witness—look, he is baptizing, and all are going to him." John answered, "A person cannot receive even one thing unless it is given him from heaven. You yourselves bear me witness, that I said, 'I am not the Christ, but I have been sent before him.'
>
> John 3:26-28

This is one of the best examples of someone who understood the importance of avoiding the pitfalls of distraction. The first distraction the Pharisees confronted John with was dissuasion by comparison. It was if they were saying, "Hey John, you know that young preacher that was with you, that you baptized and endorsed, now he's got his own following."

The implication here is, the one that you testified of and endorsed, now he's taking over. In their mind, John should have been outraged at Jesus' audacity. Then they took it to the next level. "And he's copying your techniques, by baptizing and on top of it, he's baptizing more people than you. What you got to say about that? You gonna take that lying down?"

However, John, full of wisdom and the Spirit, replied, "A person can receive only what is given them from heaven." In other words, John was saying, "This is not my program, these are not my people, and I don't own the rights to baptism. And most importantly, quit trying to compare me with the Messiah, because I already told you, 'I am not the Messiah.' I know my role and purpose. I was sent here ahead of him to prepare the way of the Lord." John's retort was right on target. The only way to avoid the pitfalls of distraction is to know your purpose.

Do What God Tells You to Do

In order to get it right on fulfilling your purpose, let's approach it from the negative aspect—what you are not placed at a church to do. You are not there to grow the church, nor are you there to make a name for yourself. Neither are you there to increase the budget, or to see more people walk down the aisle, but you are there to do what God tells you to do. You are there to serve His purpose, not yours. You are there to fulfill His will, not your own agenda.

Why is knowing your purpose so important? Because it is so easy for pastors to get caught up in the growth of churches that we set priorities based on our own agenda. As a result, when our plans are not coming together as we thought or not growing at the speed we anticipated, then discouragement and frustration set in. Once discouragement and frustration set in, that seeps into how we manage the church and how we treat the people of whom God has given us the oversight. Our attitude becomes harsh and critical, and we end up teaching and preaching from the basis of a bitter heart, all because we have unrealistic expectations that are not coming to fruition. What ought to matter most is God's approval and how you love the people you shepherd. If I may add, what has contributed to success in ministry for me has been my reliance on God and my love for His people. The old adage is true, "People will not care how much you know until they see how much you care."

We begin to battle an enemy of our own creation, but by extension we end up fighting against God and the purpose He has for that church—the epitome of a battle that cannot be won.

Pastors who find themselves in this situation become stressed and regretful, taking their misgivings out on the people, when from the beginning all they had to do was be faithful and do what God had called them to do. As John the Baptist told the Pharisees, no man can receive anything unless it is given to him by heaven. If God wants to grow the church—He'll add to it. If He wants more people walking down the aisles—He'll send them. If He wants budgets to grow—He'll add the increase.

In 1 Corinthians Paul had to rebuke the church because they were getting caught up in following personalities; they were comparing one to the other and had even thrown Paul into the fray. Therefore, he asked, "Was Paul crucified for you?" In the third chapter Paul goes on to say:

> What then is Apollos? What is Paul? Servants through whom you believed, as the Lord assigned to each. I planted, Apollos watered, but God gave the growth. So neither he who plants nor he who waters is anything, but only God who gives the growth.
>
> 1 Corinthians 3:5-7

The size of the church shouldn't matter. The budget shouldn't matter. Serving as God's servants is what matters. Every size of church needs a pastor who can be used by God right where they are. Faithfulness to God must be our goal. Serve in your purpose, be faithful where you are, and don't compare yourself to the Joneses.

CHAPTER 5

YOU'RE NOT THE EXPERT—IT'S NOT YOUR CHURCH

"Give your servant therefore an understanding mind to govern your people, that I may discern between good and evil, for who is able to govern this your great people?" It pleased the Lord that Solomon had asked this."
1 Kings 3:9-10

One of the issues that many young pastors struggle with, particularly after completing seminary, is thinking that they are the expert. They've got it all figured out and have all of the answers. I liken this to a military officer who has just completed the academy tasked with leading soldiers into war, having himself only fought in computer-simulated battles. He brings with him classroom research and theoretical tactics but has no experience, yet he thinks he's the expert. As one World War II general put it, no plan survives the battlefield—meaning what looks good on paper and in the classroom might not suffice to meet the challenge real life presents.

The new pastor's outlook is usually unrealistically bright. In his mind he has a plan to fix everything that is broken. He seems to be under the impression that no one at the church had any sense or understanding of how things "really work" until he got there. However, here is something that every pastor needs to know: you do not have the sense to lead God's people. Not only is this thinking arrogant, but it is also foolish. The fact is that only God knows how to lead His people.

I opened this chapter with 1 Kings 3, where Solomon has a conversation with God in a dream. In verse 5, God says to Solomon, "Ask for whatever you want me to give you." However, Solomon does not answer the question with a list of gimmies, but he responds with the following self-assessment and then a very wise request.

> And now, O LORD my God, you have made your servant king in place of David my father, although I am but a little child. I do not know how to go out or come in. And your servant is in the midst of your people whom you have chosen, a great people, too many to be numbered or counted for multitude. Give your servant therefore an understanding mind to govern your people, that I may discern between good and evil, for who is able to govern this your great people?" It pleased the Lord that Solomon had asked this.
>
> 1 Kings 3:7-10

Solomon's self-assessment is remarkable. Being able to rightly assess yourself puts you in the position of making the right inquiries, but you hastily make a wrong decision. Solomon assesses, "I am too naïve to know how to do this job on my own." In other words, even though Solomon watched his father David rule, he realizes that he is no expert. He totally understands that he does not have the mental or spiritual capacity to rule the "people that God has chosen, a great people, too numerous to count or number."

Put yourself in Solomon's shoes, where God comes to you concerning your next pastoral assignment, saying, "Ask whatever you would like me to do for you concerning pastoring this church." Would you ask for more members, more money, more time, or to get rid of obstinate members and challenges? You see, if you did ask for those things, you would be asking "off purpose." It is not the pastor's purpose to accomplish those secondary things. Solomon had it right. Seeking God for the wisdom to fulfill the purpose God has for that congregation is where your heart and mind should be focused. Solomon confessed that he didn't know what he was doing and therefore needed God's help to avoid focusing on the wrong things and completely messing up this assignment.

As a pastor, you have to humble yourself and admit that on your own, seminary degree and all, you do not have the wisdom to know how to deal with the people God has assigned to you. You must remind yourself: I do not know these people's history. I cannot read these people's minds. I cannot perfectly assess these people's gifts and abilities. I do not know what problems they will face tomorrow. I simply do not have enough knowledge to lead God's people. Therefore, God, I need your help.

THESE ARE NOT YOUR PEOPLE

Another salient point that Solomon acknowledges, found in verse 8, is that "your servant is here among *the people you have chosen.*" Solomon understands that these are not his people, but the people God has chosen. Another passage of Scripture that touches on this subject is found in Acts, when Paul makes a passionate speech to the elders at Ephesus just prior to his departure for Rome, Paul declares:

> Pay careful attention to yourselves and to all the flock, in which the Holy Spirit has made you overseers, to care for the church of God, which he obtained with his own blood.
>
> Acts 20:28

From this verse, you should be able to see that there is only one person that should be using possessive terms when it comes to the church—that person is God. These are not your people. You did not purchase anyone with your own blood. You see, when something is yours, you are free to do with it whatever you please. You make statements such as: *This is my church. These are my people. This is my vision.* And so on. We pastors are guilty of saying this all the time. But not only are we saying it, we actually run the church as if it were "my church."

However, make no mistake about it, that is a spirit of pride. All you have to do is go back to what Paul declared: "Keep watch over yourselves and all the flock of which the Holy Spirit has made you overseers." *Keep watch over yourselves;* in other words, don't get it confused. Don't let a spirit of pride step in. Know that you are primarily a servant, an under-shepherd, called to lead *the flock of which the Holy Spirit has made you overseers.* God made you the *overseer.* If you walk into a congregation as a pastor, it is God by the Holy Spirit who has placed you there. You are the *overseer*, not the *owner*. This is God's flock, not yours.

To emphasize the fact that the church belongs to God, Paul states, "Be shepherds of the church of God, which He bought with His own blood." As the refrain of the old Gospel song says, "Jesus paid it all. All to Him I owe…." How then can we act as if though this is *our* church, or think these are *our* people. We purchased nothing. We only serve by the grace of God. We are unprofitable servants rendering our reasonable service. The fact that God saves us and allows us to serve Him in ministry is more than we deserve. We are on a much better footing for success when we realize that we are not the experts and that these are not our people.

As we return to Solomon, there is a final point worth emphasizing. God was very pleased with Solomon for asking for wisdom to fulfill his purpose rather than asking for superficial things. Therefore, God gave him the wisdom he requested, more than any other man before or after him. On top of that, God blessed him all with the riches and material wealth that he didn't ask for.

What should we learn from this? You don't have to ask God for a church bigger than the Joneses church down the street. You don't have to ask for more members or money. You don't have to ask for fame or prestige. All you have to do is what God tells you to do, and He will handle the rest. If He wants to send more members, He'll send them. If it is more finances, He'll send the money. If it's church growth, He'll increase it. If He wants you to have significant influence, He'll bestow it. At the end of the day, it's His church, and these are God's people that He saved for His glory—not yours.

If you need wisdom to navigate through a church conflict, seek the Lord's face about what He wants you to do. Ask Him to do what needs to be done in the people. God's power is your greatest asset. Do not try to take matters into your own hands, because God can accomplish what you are not able to do. Seek Him to guide you as He makes changes. As one preacher once said, "What the grace of God cannot do, the grave will. You lead and feed. Leave the rest to God."

If the power of God and the effectiveness of any ministry are going to come to pass, it is not going to happen in your might nor will it happen in your strength; it's only going to happen through the power of God. You do not know it all. You cannot say it all. You cannot do it all. You must be dependent upon God to get it done. You *are not* the expert.

CHAPTER 6

THE ISSACHAR PRINCIPLE—LEADING THROUGH CHANGE

Of Issachar, men who had understanding of the times,
to know what Israel ought to do, 200 chiefs, and all their
kinsmen under their command.
1 Chronicles 12:32

Not long ago, an aging pastor of a metropolitan church hired a new youth minister who was able to introduce some innovative youth programming that attracted Millennials and Centennials (aka Generation Z). Though the numbers on the membership roll were increasing, the pastor did not see a correlating rise in weekly contributions. Therefore, the senior pastor called in the youth pastor and insisted he start emphasizing to these new members the importance of giving. The youth pastor suggested the pastor introduce new ways of giving that are familiar to this generation, which typically does not write checks or carry much cash. The youth pastor suggested utilizing text-to-give and developing some interactive applications that would get out the messaging and provide content that would reach this generation.

The pastor was unrelenting in his opposition to "modernize" and introduce all this "technology stuff," and insisted there is nothing better than cold, hard cash in the collection plate. Then the pastor uttered seven words that have the potential to kill any church on the cusp of change: "We've never done it that way before." The youth minister was put off by this because the pastor was not only ignoring his advice, but also ignoring the reality of how young people conduct financial transactions today. The youth pastor also pointed out many churches receive a significant percentage of their weekly contributions this way.

So the pastor resorted to what had worked in the past and began hammering tithing and offerings from the pulpit to a generation that carries little cash and increasingly does everything electronically and on their smartphones. Soon, a rift developed between the pastor and the youth minister over this and other issues. Each time the youth minister tried to introduce something up-to-date that would benefit the church, he hit a brick wall with the pastor. Eventually, the youth minister became disillusioned and left the ministry. After that happened, the church's youth membership declined, but the church's dwindling budget and membership remained.

Here is the question: *Was there a missed opportunity here?* How did the pastor's insecurity and failure to understand the times in which we now live cause him to miss out on ministering to a willing, searching and inquisitive generation in whose lives technology plays an important part? Whether you like it or not, the fact is technology is here to stay. To hold up progress over the idea that we've never done it that way before could be a costly mistake. In order to be effective in a 21st century church, you must know the times and be willing to learn and lead through change.

THE SONS OF ISSACHAR

Of the twelve tribes of Israel, Issachar is a somewhat enigmatic tribe. Issachar, the progenitor of the tribe, was the ninth son of Jacob, and the fifth borne by Leah. Not much is known about this tribe, as there is little documented in the Scriptures about them. However, in 1 Chronicles 12:32, it is said the sons of Issachar were men who understood the times and had knowledge of what Israel should do, knowing when it was time to adhere to new leadership.

Matthew Henry gives an interesting insight into the skill and sagacity of the Issacharites:

> They were men of great skill above any of their neighbors, men that had understanding of the times, to know

what Israel ought to do. They understood the natural times, could discern the face of the sky, were weather-wise, could advise their neighbors in the proper times for plowing, sowing, reaping, etc. Or the ceremonial times, the times appointed for the solemn feasts...[5]

What can pastors of the 21st century learn from an ancient tribe of Israel? The importance of knowing or having someone who knows the times advising you can be absolutely critical in your decision making as a leader. A great idea before its time is a bad idea today. Moving too soon or too late can make the difference between success and failure. Everything is about timing; therefore, you must know the times.

We must be very careful about initiating plans and projects we undertake without careful discernment. Speaking parabolically, Jesus gave this admonition and warning when He instructed:

> For which of you, desiring to build a tower, does not first sit down and count the cost, whether he has enough to complete it? Otherwise, when he has laid a foundation and is not able to finish, all who see it begin to mock him, saying, 'This man began to build and was not able to finish.
>
> Luke 14:28-30

To put that in today's language, it wouldn't be wise to start a building fund on "faith" without the proper financing secured while the economy is sliding and recession is looming. We have to be wise enough to discern the times and count up the costs of our decisions.

THE ART OF LEADING THROUGH CHANGE

First of all, no one likes change. More likely than not, people prefer to maintain the status quo, keeping things just as they have always been. It's easy. It's the path of least resistance. Therefore, how change is initiated is of great importance and must be handled with the utmost consideration to those who are going to be exposed to it.

Too often, new pastors want to come in and quickly establish their territory by bringing in sweeping reforms. As I covered in the last chapter, this mindset is often attributed to believing they are the expert. However, before you change anything, you must first survey the congregational landscape. You must discern the timing of when to make certain changes. You must also understand that before the people will buy in to the changes you are proposing, you must first win over the support of the key power players within the organizational structure. That means you cannot make the mistake of trying to change everything. You must be discerning. There are some good things that should stay in place. If something works and is effective, then keep it. It's important to leave something that's recognizable; something that the people can hold on to that is familiar. In other words, be willing to compromise. Do not be so quick to shut down others' opinions and input. Avoid alienating people who may bring good ideas to the table that you hadn't considered. Remember, you are the new kid on the block, and you have the disadvantage of "not knowing." Therefore, you must discover how it is that you can serve these people and meet them where they are.

There are core principles unique to every congregation that should remain intact. You don't want to throw the baby out with the bath water. That would be a sure recipe for disruption and dissent. Remember, your intentions are to bring positive change for the good. You don't want the changes you are proposing to become a point of contention or become a distraction. Be reassuring. Foster sensitivity. Yes, we may need to change how we get there and when we get there. We may also need to change the presentation and the container, but the message, the theology and the fundamentals will remain the same. Leave people with enough familiarity in order for them to be more accepting of incorporating new changes.

RECOGNIZING THE TIMES ABOUT YOU

We all change. Whether the change happens because of personal experience or because it is forced upon us through circumstance, change is inevitable. What is most important is how do we adapt? How do we lead through it? Years ago, when I served at my first church, I had formulated how things would be at my next church. In a sense, I created a template for my future leadership. However, the inherent weakness in that was the things I learned at the previous ministry were based upon what I saw. What I saw was limited. That meant what I knew was limited. All I knew about ministry came from what I had experienced at the last church. What I saw on the pulpit and in the boardroom was the experiential totality of what I brought to my first pastoral assignment.

However, after the first few years at my new church, I saw I could start doing things my own way as opposed to how my previous pastor had done them. It was at that point that I realized that much of what I had witnessed in my past experiences that served as my template for ministry did not have to be done the same way. My template, based upon the past ministry, was not the best approach for the new ministry. There is more than one way to achieve the same result. Therefore, I had to recognize the times in me. I had to confront my own misconceptions about bringing my old ways to a new situation.

It takes courage to examine yourself. You must know the times and understand the first changes that might need to be instituted may be within you. You must be willing to institute the better way that works for everyone, not just for you. It takes self-discernment to know when change is good and necessary, even when it goes against what you thought was the best way. Before you can effectively lead through change, be sure you know the times around you and within you. Pray for discernment and the tactical know-how to implement change.

CHAPTER 7

IT'S HIS VISION, NOT YOURS

Where there is no vision [no redemptive revelation of God], the people perish; but he who keeps the law [of God, which includes that of man]—blessed (happy, fortunate, and enviable) is he.
Proverbs 29:18, AMP

A question that is often asked is, *What is your vision for the church?* Another way of asking the same thing is, *What are your plans for the future direction of the church?* However, innate in the question is an inherent problem that begins with the adjective *your*. The definition of *your* is *relating to you or yourself or yourselves especially as possessor or possessors.* However, when it comes to the church the Lord has purchased with His own blood and appointed pastors as overseers, is it appropriate for a church leader to seek his own vision?

In the Amplified Version of Proverbs 29:18, I like how the nuances of the passage are emphasized that other English translations miss. The "a" clause of the passage reads, "Where there is no vision [no redemptive revelation of God], the people perish." It is the words in the brackets that bring important clarity to the concept of "vision." The word "vision" is equated to *the redemptive revelation of God.* Understanding that when it comes to "vision" it is the redemptive revelation of God that is really in view, the most important question is, where does the word *your* come into play?

Some years ago when I was interviewing to become pastor of a church, one of the questions the committee asked was, "What is your vision for the church?" I assumed they expected me to have done my due diligence by researching the history of the church, and familiarizing myself with some of the church's current goals and aspirations. Therefore, they would have been anxious to learn my thoughts on what direction I thought the church should be going. However, I did not give them the answer they expected. My answer to the question, "If you were to become pastor, what is your vision for the church?" was "I don't know."

Initially, they were startled by that answer. However, I quickly explained the reason I answered the way that I did. My explanation was: "Today, I am not the pastor. If God were to see fit to make me the pastor, I would go to Him and ask Him what is His vision for this church." The salient point that must be emphasized here is that it should always be about God's vision for the church, which the pastor is sent to execute. A pastor is like an ambassador sent to a foreign land to execute the agenda of the nation from which he was sent. An ambassador is not there to promote his own agenda, but to implement the agenda of the one that appointed him.

Who has the best vision? The answer is simple—the one who can see the best, and the one who can see the farthest. The one who can declare the end from the beginning. The one who has the power to make all of His counsel stand. The one who has all power in His hands, is all-knowing and who fills all time and space. The one who knows the hearts of men, and can see in the darkest of places. He has the plan, and He has the vision. How effective a pastor will be is in direct correlation to how closely he follows the leading of God.

When a pastor follows God's vision, it is God who is responsible for fulfilling what it is He called you to do. However, when it's your vision, then you have to plead to God for His help with something He did not authorize. That's not the place you want to be. There are countless examples of pastors led by ego and pride who have ruined people and churches in pursuit of something God did not tell them to do. Your vision is not as good as God's. God knows everything about your church, about the people and about you. You don't know what is going to happen in the next five minutes, let alone the next five years.

One of the greatest skills a pastor can possess is learning how to wait on the Lord's leading and follow His directions, lest you smite the rock twice and fall short of entering the Promised Land. Moses was Israel's greatest leader, having come through the Exodus, forty years of wandering in the wilderness, seeing miracle after miracle and witnessing the demonstrations of deliverance by God's mighty hand. But somewhere along the way, Moses had a different vision for God's people, and he failed to do as God told him to do. Moses let his anger get in the way. The minute he did that, he was off God's vision and had switched to his own, where he felt justified to deviate from God's plan.

Whenever a pastor deviates from God's vision or plan and reverts to his own vision, he has put himself in opposition to God's plan. That's a dangerous place to be. You cannot expect to have a successful vision when you are in opposition to the One with the provision. Moses is not the one who made water flow from a rock. God did. The people were about to turn on Moses because they had no water and faced dying of thirst. Only God had a plan for that situation in which Moses on his own would not have survived. People will quickly turn on their leaders. This is why you have to depend on God and do this thing the way He has determined. No pastor can lead people on his own. These are not your people. You are not the expert. And no matter what seminary you graduate from, you are not smart enough.

God told Moses to speak to the rock, but that didn't satisfy Moses' anger at the people adequately enough. So Moses reverted to his own vision, and smote the rock twice as he told the people a thing or two in the process. That was not God's plan, and Moses, Israel's greatest leader, paid the price—he died before reaching the Promised Land, only beholding it with his eyes. In other words, his vision let him see it, but did not let him experience it. Who had the better vision? God. Remember, it's not your vision—it's the Lord's.

Chapter 8

People Matter

Understanding Those Whom You Lead

The beginning of wisdom is: Acquire wisdom; And with all
your acquiring, get understanding.
Proverbs 4:7, NASB

A recent graduate from seminary got the opportunity to teach his first Sunday school lesson. The new minster couldn't wait to share what was one of his burning passions, on the subject of soteriology. He figured he would dazzle his students with some five-dollar theological words concerning the doctrine of election such as the term *superlapserianism*. After the class, he was feeling very impressed with himself. He stayed focused, stuck to his outline and got through all the material before the class was over. However, one of the church mothers came up to him and said, "Young man, that was some lesson you just taught, but next time could you teach something that the rest of us can understand?"

This scenario brings to mind an old cliché that has a lot of truth: "People don't care what you know until they know that you care." One of the biggest obstacles college graduates face is the one they erect—thinking they have all the answers. In all fairness, it's not totally their fault because they just graduated from an institution that has educated them through a rigorous learning process. Therefore, they're oozing with information that is looking for a place to be deposited. So, with sheepskin in hand, they are itching for the opportunity to share some of that good old education with anyone who will listen. However, in doing so, they may actually be starting this race off on the wrong foot. Why? Because people are not impressed by what you know. Your knowledge of ecclesiology, eschatology, anthropology or soteriology won't breach the "do you really care" barrier.

If you are going to serve people, they have to be more than repositories for your classroom training. They are not some control group you can collect data on to conduct experiments. These are God's people with hearts and minds who need to be developed into spiritual maturity. If it were just a matter of transfer of information to achieve that, pastoring would be much simpler. However, the people whom you will pastor are complex individuals with their own way of thinking and doing things with their own unique set of good, bad and ugly. But before they entrust you with their heart, they must be assured you genuinely care about them.

PEOPLE MUST MATTER

I once heard a pastor make a comment about members, money and parking spaces. The way he saw it was that for every parking space, there was one tithe-paying family. The average tithe-paying family brings in a couple grand annually in tithes. Therefore, multiply each parking space by a couple grand and you have a way of anticipating revenues. Want more revenue? Have plenty of parking. Though it is true parking spaces are important, I use this example because the last thing you want to do is see God's people through the lens of statistical analysis. People are more than just numbers on a roll, members in the pews or dollars in the offering basket. The people have to matter to you. It doesn't matter what you know. It doesn't matter how well you preach. Above all, people must know you care about them. However, the key to caring about someone is taking the time to understand them.

In Proverbs 4:7, the wise man teaches, "Wisdom *is* the principal thing; *therefore* get wisdom: and with all thy getting get understanding." Understanding is different than knowing. I know a jet can fly, but I have no understanding of how it flies. Like passengers on a commuter train, you can see the same people every morning and exchange greetings every day. But other than that, you have no understanding of who they are. You have no idea of where they are coming from, and you have no idea of where they are going. You have no idea what they have been through. You have no idea of what makes them tick, their likes and dislikes. You have no knowledge of their history, nor about the things that are most important to them. But in that sense you could still say: I know that person. I see them every day. They get on the train at the same stop at a certain time. They get off at the same stop every day. We spend time on the train together, and sometimes we even sit together. However, I have no understanding of who they are. Knowing someone superficially is fine for your morning commute, but as a pastor of a church, you need to understand that if a person doesn't know you care, you won't get very far with them.

KNOWING THE POWER PLAYERS

In America, we elect a new president every four years. It's always amazing to hear candidates promoting what they are going to do when they get into office. However, as well intentioned as the candidate may be, if elected, his agenda will go nowhere if he doesn't have key power players in the Congress and Senate backing him. Each congressman and senator has a loyal constituency in their state or district, who are going to follow the lead of the ones they elected to represent them. Behind each congressman and senator there are millions of voters.

Though the institution of the church is different than national and state politics, the politics in church is often very similar. In a church where the pastor makes all the decisions, it is an autocratic structure. In a congregational structure, members in good standing vote on important issues, even when it comes to the pastor himself. For example, in the A.M.E. (African Methodist Episcopal) churches, their pastors have to be voted in by the congregation every year. And whenever you have voting, you have politics. Therefore, churches can be autocratic, democratic or somewhere in between.

Each church has a unique set of interpersonal dynamics and congregational attributes. There are those people who only attend on special Sundays: Easter, Mother's Day and Christmas. There are those who come religiously every week but never get involved beyond Sunday attendance. There are those who are more committed; they attend midweek Bible class and are more likely to connect service in the church to serving God. You also have those who attend church who seek prestige and status, and want to be seen. However, there are those who are more dominant and are able to bring others under their sphere of influence; these are called power players. They may be an associate pastor, a minister, deacon or trustee, a generous contributor, a local politician, or a member of a family that has long standing in the church. Power players tend to carry a sense of privilege and entitlement because of their status among the congregants.

As a new pastor, you must approach your role realistically. You have to understand there were dynamics and an infrastructure that existed long before you arrived. The infrastructure may need fixing. How they have been doing things might need correcting, but it is important to see these things are not occurring in a vacuum. There are people behind these things. So when you say you want to change a long-standing practice, what you are really saying is you need to change the people behind it.

It would be a mistake to think you are totally in control simply because you carry the title of pastor. You have to earn people's respect in order for them to trust your leadership. In other words, people have to know you care for them and that you have identified the power players. Whether for good or bad, power players are influencers. Power players have other people's ears. People come to power players to seek their advice and to get a second opinion about what's going on in the church.

A pastor needs to realize that, in reality, they don't pastor everyone in the church. What I mean by that is, there is a power player in the church who has more influence over that individual than the pastor does. So it is important that you understand, if you can pastor the power players, then you have a better chance of pastoring the people who come to them. Another way of looking at that concept is to pastor the power players until you become the pastor over people whom they lead.

There are a few questions that are asked among the people about the pastor that will never be asked directly of the pastor: How do you like this pastor's manner? How do you like his leadership style? How do you like the way he preaches and teaches? Are you onboard with the pastor's new vision, and are you going to support it? How do you feel about the pastor's new plans for church expansion?

These are some of the questions the power players are asked all the time. And how they answer these questions can determine how the ones who listen to them will respond. If a power player responds, "No, I think that is a bad idea," the pastor's attempt at persuasion from the pulpit can fall on deaf ears in the congregation, and his agenda could be dead on arrival, leaving the pastor to figure out what's wrong.

This is why the new pastor must understand the people whom he is leading. It may take years before people let you into their heart—if they ever do. It has been said it normally takes a new pastor from five to seven years before he truly becomes the pastor in the hearts and minds of the people. In general, established church members do not come to church because of who the pastor is, they come to the church as an institution. They come to that church because this is the church their family has attended for years, sometimes generations. Their loyalty is to the church, not necessarily to the pastor. If there comes a pastor whom the establishment members do not like, they become part of the impetus and force to get that pastor out.

Therefore, when you come to a church, take time to understand the people. Find out their interests. Determine what makes them tick. What are their concerns? What motivates them? What persuades them? It is important to ascertain the context of a church's history and membership before you try to make any major decisions.

Another important aspect of congregational dynamics presents itself in the church plant. Whenever a minister has started the church, obviously there are no previous pastors or old members with which to contend. However, being a church plant does present a unique set of challenges. Though many of the members may be new Christians who require more attention in discipleship, it's the members who come in from other churches who can bring problems with them. Experienced Christians who join new churches often come with biases and issues such as church hurt, discipline and subordination issues, not being teachable or having an agenda. Many may have a "get in on the ground floor"mentality that is not spiritually motivated, rather an opportunity to become a power player and exploit the inexperienced pastor.

Though the pastor of a church plant rejoices over anyone who walks through the doors, he must also be discerning. Questions such as *Why did you leave your past church of ten years* need to be answered. People like this may be just the people you need whom the Lord has sent to you, but they may also be wolves in sheep's clothing. This is why in any context, it is imperative to understand those you lead, while seeking God's face for discernment.

Chapter 9

Develop a Clear Ministry Strategy

Strategy: the way in which a business, government, or other organization carefully plans its actions over a period of time to improve its position and achieve what it wants.
The Cambridge Dictionary

Strategy, strategy, strategy. Everyone wants to get a hold of the "winning strategy." Nowadays, there are so many self-help seminars that tout the 1-2-3 or A-B-Cs of success in various fields and pursuits. However, many of these are nothing more than cleverly disguised marketing schemes designed to part those looking for a quick fix from their money. All these gatherings do is capitalize on the hype, which is quickly deflated once you return to the real world. It's like the cheap pair of shoes that seem to fit in the store, but once you get them home, you realize they are too tight.

However, successful strategies do not occur in a vacuum nor by osmosis. Strategies don't just happen or come prepackaged and ready-made. An effective strategy must be developed with unique specifics in mind. In other words, there is no one-size-fits all for strategic success. Success is a calculated series of predetermined steps, with specific goals and objectives with measurable outcomes. It is possible that a person could become a multimillionaire with the purchase of a two-dollar Lotto ticket. However, that wealth will take wing and fly away if you do not develop a strategy to maintain it.

I twice attended a conference hosted by celebrated pastor and author Rick Warren of Saddleback Church in Lake Forest, California. I was absolutely amazed at the enormity of this mega-church that has fifteen locations in California, and one in Berlin, Germany, Buenos Aires, Argentina, Hong Kong and Santa Rosa, Philippines. The weekly attendance is over 22,000. According to their website, they have 168 ministries dispersed over twelve categories such as Outreach, On Campus, Family, Care and eight others. What is interesting is the category with the largest number of ministries is Outreach, with thirty-four different auxiliary ministries. Each of the thirty-four ministries under this outreach category has its own focus and purpose statement.

A church of this size and magnitude has to employ an effective strategy for growth and maintenance or it would simply collapse under its own weight. Whenever pastors attend conferences, you immediately get the sense that "Saddleback has it right." "If I employ the same ministry strategies at my church they have there, then we would experience similar exponential growth." But is that true?

This is what Rick Warren, author of *The Purpose Driven Church* and *The Purpose Driven Life*, said during one of his conferences about this subject: "The strategy that we employ is *a* strategy. We have some great concepts here, but I don't want you to go back to your church and attempt to mimic everything you see happening here at Saddleback because it's not going to work. By all means, use what works for you and throw out the rest."

As I covered in the last chapter, you must understand the people you are leading. You must know the idiosyncrasies, history and organizational culture of the church you are aspiring to move forward. Once you have a good grip on that, you can start developing a tailor-made strategy for the growth of the church you are pastoring.

Start with the overall vision God gives you for the church, then evaluate where you are now as a church. Once you clearly understand where you are and who you are, then it's time to plan your structure and strategies to facilitate getting to the end result.

After you have clearly planned a method that contains structure, which makes it easier to understand and follow, you will need to get those in the church to buy in. Habakkuk 2:2 says, And the LORD answered me: "Write the vision; make it plain on tablets, so he may run who reads it." The ministry strategy must make biblical sense, be clear and progressive in order for others to grab it and run with it.

DEVELOPING DISCIPLES

In 1 Peter, we find these encouraging words where the apostle likens new Christians as being babies in Christ. "Like newborn babies, crave pure spiritual milk, so that by it you may grow up in your salvation" (1 Peter 2:2, NIV). This metaphor is by no means critical, but merely building upon the spiritual reality that a true Christian has to be transformed by new birth. Therefore, no matter what age a person is when they become saved, everyone starts out as a babe in Christ. The term babe or baby implies the necessity of development, as any child requires.

As in the natural, so it is in the spiritual. One of the many challenges encountered in child rearing is keeping children engaged in positive, enriching activities. Without appropriate engagement, children become easily distracted and vulnerable to negative behaviors. Children do much better in their development when they have structured activities in which to engage. Where there is no structure, life for a child becomes confusing because they do not know what to expect or how to adjust. However, when structure is in place, and the child knows what to expect and what is expected of them, you have a most-positive environment for development and growth. The same is true in a church setting concerning the development of babes in Christ. This process is called discipleship. Someone must invest time and effort into the development of future generations of Christians to prepare them for a fulfilling and productive life in Christ.

As I pointed out earlier, Saddleback's largest ministry category is Outreach, with an amazing thirty-four ministries under that banner. By the very nature of the term itself, *outreach* means exactly that, ministries that reach out beyond the four walls of the church. Much of a church's growth will come from effectively taking the church's mission and resources and activating them in the community to effect positive change and win souls for the kingdom of God. However, before you can have a dynamic impact in the community, you must develop a ministry strategy for developing disciples who become vision carriers.

It is not my purpose here to tell you how to develop a program for dynamic and effective discipleship, but that it should be a principal area of focus. Without a way to make disciples, the ministry will eventually stagnate. What is needed is a mechanism that will support perpetuity. Just because a pastor retires, gets fired or expires, the ministry should not collapse. When you fail to make disciples and the ministry is centered around an autocratic personality, you are setting the ministry up for failure.

The Newness Wears Off

In countless churches, an altar call for souls to come to Christ is made every Sunday. The metaphoric phrase typically used for this is called "opening the doors of the church." Here is where individuals come to Christ or to join the church. However, it doesn't take long being in ministry to discover churches have revolving doors. As readily as people come in through the front door, they can also leave through the back door. Therefore, pastors come up with all sorts of techniques that often boil down to marketing tactics to retain members because eventually the newness wears off. The excitement of joining a church can soon give way to a spirit of apathy, as church services are perceived as mundane or perfunctory.

Speaking on this subject, I once heard a well-known pastor give insight on membership retention. The pastor stated you can only keep people so long with "a message." He found that to be true when a smaller ministry with a less-known pastor came to town, and many of his members went over to the other ministry. Being curious as to what they were offering that his ministry was not, he found out they were engaging people by letting them function in the church. Not necessarily on the pulpit, but in the Ministry of Helps and inviting people to engage their skills and talents in support of the church and its mission. By doing so, the people reached the buy-in point quickly, because they saw themselves as a part of the ministry, not just mere members coming to hear a message. Mere members are easy to shake loose because they have no real investment in the church beyond simply going to church. When a new and exciting ministry pops up where these members can work, they are attracted to the new church. The fact is everyone wants to feel they are a part of something great, know they are appreciated and have a voice by way of participation. Church for them has to be more than coming to hear a message on Sunday morning.

The newness eventually wears off. The exciting messages become mundane, and fads and the fantasy of Sunday soon fade away. However, if you are developing disciples and engaging people's skills and talents, they become invested and won't be as susceptible to being pulled away as soon as the new church in town opens its doors.

The church is to be a family. The initial goal is to get people connected to the church family and give them a sense of belonging as soon as possible. Your job as a church leader is to ensure the new people coming to the ministry feel connected. Connection is what helps close the back door.

Therefore, you need to develop a strategy as to how you are going to make disciples. How are you going to develop people "on purpose" who meet the needs of the church today and in the future? Failing to do so will be detrimental to the church. Like the developing child, people need structure. Without structure, people will soon get lost and become bored and dissatisfied, causing them to be ineffective, nonparticipating members who are easily siphoned off.

When people come to a church, they are trying to answer the "what's." *What is* this ministry about? *What is* this church doing? And so on. It is answering the "what's" that keeps people wanting to attend your church. Therefore, it is imperative to develop strategies that work especially in the area of discipleship. At the end of the day, a church's primarily purpose is to win souls to Christ and enact strategies for growth and maturity.

CHAPTER 10

DESIGN FOR CONTEXTUAL SUCCESS

What does success mean to you? While pondering this question, I'm looking not so much for the functional definition of success, but for the contextual definition. According to Dictionary.com, success is defined as *the favorable or prosperous termination of attempts or endeavors; the accomplishment of one's goals*. This is the objective definition for everyone. However, there is a subjective aspect to success that must be defined within the context of circumstance. You cannot attempt to convince people who can barely afford a bus pass for public transportation as to why they need to buy a Mercedes Benz. Or if you are a retail store owner, you must know how to stock products based upon the demographic that patronizes your store. Trying to sell air conditioners at the North Pole would not be a successful endeavor. Therefore, success and the context in which it comes to fruition are important issues that must be identified and mastered. In order to experience what Joshua 1:8 describes as "good success," it must be designed contextually.

THE DETERMENT OF EXTERNAL INFLUENCES

Among the most formidable barriers to success are hopelessness and despair. Hopelessness and despair are often the result of people believing the wrong message about themselves and their future. For example, in Exodus, before the Children of Israel were to go into the Promised Land, twelve spies were sent out to conduct surveillance and to bring back a report on what they saw so Israel could develop a strategy to go in and possess the land. However, only two of these spies came back with a positive, "we can take it" report, whereas ten of the spies came back with negative reports saying, "It's not accomplishable. They are giants, we are grasshoppers." What the ten negative voices reported dashed the hopes of the people, and they lost faith and the desire to possess the fertile and fruitful land promised to them by the Lord. As a result, instead of possessing the land, Israel wandered in the wilderness for forty years. Why? Because of the influence of the negative report. How they saw themselves was altered after accepting a dissuading report from an external source.

We hear these external reports all time. If you believed all the reports of the talking heads on cable news, you wouldn't have enough optimism left to get out of bed in the morning. However, no matter how much criticism the naysayers spout, a pastor who knows how to design for contextual success cannot be stopped. A remarkable case in point of a pastor who knew how to capitalize on the contextual is Reverend Johnny Ray Youngblood, Pastor Emeritus of St. Paul Community Baptist Church of Brooklyn, New York.

The *New York Times* once described the community surrounding St. Paul Community Baptist Church as "one of God's Alcatrazes that had been dismissed by city politicians as a violent wasteland.[6]" Certainly, many of the residents of this impoverished community imbibed and believed that negative report as they survived day by day in a so-called hopeless contextual circumstance. However, what the naysayers dismissed as hopeless, Pastor Youngblood saw as a diamond in the rough. He didn't come in with some unattainable lofty ideas, but took contextually appropriate steps in the right direction that would lead to transformed lives and a totally revitalized community.

Within a decade, Pastor Youngblood focused on the men of the community to instill hope and possibility to those who had been accustomed to gangs, drugs, death and jail. He inspired them to turn their energy inward, and to rebuild themselves and their community. Youngblood's efforts were so successful the ministry grew to over five thousand members, transforming a wasteland into an oasis.

Pastor Youngblood would never have been so successful if he had accentuated and perpetuated the perceptions of those who didn't care to understand the context of the people's circumstances. No, he had to understand where they were, and work with them from that point in order to pull them up higher. He realized that if men were the source of many of the ills plaguing the community, then the men would have to be transformed by the power of God and through a renewed mind; not employing a wait-for-the-Promised Land mentality, but by executing a changing-your-present strategy.

As a byproduct of focusing on the men of the community, St. Paul created one of the largest male church contingencies in America, ignoring the criticisms and stereotypes commonly hurled at Black men as being corrupt and deadbeats. Youngblood's accomplishments through the congregants of St. Paul silenced the pessimism of the critics by focusing on the contextual realities of the people in order to execute a successful transformation.

St. Paul's accomplishments included constructing a school on church property, turning places where prostitution and illegal gambling operations had been conducted into family-owned businesses, and, for community youth, paid college tuition. Another huge accomplishment that became a template for future federal housing programs was the Nehemiah Housing Project, where over 2,300 affordable single-family homes were constructed in a neglected area of Brooklyn.

As we can see from what Reverend Youngblood accomplished in Brooklyn in an area considered to be a "wasteland" with people considered to be hopeless, nothing is impossible when strategies are designed from the basis of contextual success.

THE NECESSITY OF A DISCIPLESHIP PROCESS

So many people join churches every Sunday. Many of these churches have no way to assist and ensure spiritual growth for their new members. A number of people who say "I do" to Jesus on Sunday end up not attending church regularly. This retention dilemma is often due to there being no disciple development process. The reality is there is no 1-2-3 one-size-fits-all discipleship process that works within every church context. In fact, it was ministry guru Rick Warren, author of the acclaimed book *The Purpose Driven Church*, who said, "Take what you can from the purpose driven church model, and only use what will work in your context."

The Great Commission in Matthew 28:19-20 reminds us everyone is to be an evangelist. Therefore, it is important that every church has a method to grow disciples to spiritual maturity, on purpose. It should be the design from start to finish, so people don't lose focus on a logical path as to how they are to go up. Tenure as a member of a church does not guarantee how a person grows ministry. What stimulates growth is how a person understands and follows the path for spiritual development. By implementing a dynamic program for training disciples, it creates an environment for learning, teaching and training, and sending them out to make other disciples.

Whatever your path is, it needs to be logical, progressive, structured and identifiable. These elements encompass a process that you need to discover that is unique to your congregation. At the church where I pastor, we utilize a four-step process for disciple development called The Focused Church. The steps are enlisting converts, teaching disciples, training believers and sending evangelists. What you choose for your church may be different, but whatever the program you initiate, you need to have a dedicated process for how people grow up on purpose. Pastor Rick Warren uses a diamond process method from membership to magnification. However, whatever process you elect to use, ensure it is identifiable and clear and has a growth process in it.

Chapter 11

The Art of Leading People

One of the NFL's most celebrated icons, the late great Green Bay Packers coach Vince Lombardi, known for his game-winning record during his illustrious career, once stated, "Leaders aren't born, they are made. They are made by hard effort, which is the price which all of us must pay to achieve any goal which is worthwhile." This ageless quote is loaded with golden nuggets of truth and emphasizes the art of leading people.

According to *Webster's Dictionary*, an *art* is *a skill acquired by experience, study, or observation*. Here, the functional definition, Vince Lombardi's quote and the title of this chapter are all based on the same principle: Leadership is an art developed through experience and observation, and therefore, leaders are not born but made. A person can possess innate leadership qualities or characteristics, but in order to be a successful leader, one must undergo development.

One of the worst mistakes a church can make is elevating a novice into leadership too soon, or hiring someone who does not have leadership experience. In the pastoral epistles, we find this passage of Scripture addresses inexperienced leadership: "…not a new convert, so that he will not become conceited and fall into the condemnation incurred by the devil. And he must have a good reputation with those outside *the church*, so that he will not fall into reproach and the snare of the devil" (1 Timothy 3:6-7, NASB). From this passage, we see not only is it a tactical error to put in someone who has not been tried and tested in leadership, but it is also a spiritual trap that Satan can exploit. Your ego may get you in the door, but ego cannot keep you or fortify you against the weight of responsibility that inevitably presses against you once you step into the leadership role.

CAPITALIZE ON EMPIRICAL EXPERIENCE

Throughout this book, I have emphasized this motif: *Nothing beats experience*. However, in the Bible, there is much to say about the lives of great leaders such as King David. David had an encounter with calling at a young age, where God prepared him for leadership through years of adverse circumstances. Sometimes the situations David found himself in were downright diabolical, but in the long run they all worked out for his good, preparing him for leadership.

In David's case, fighting off a lion and a bear while tending sheep prepared him for the battle with Goliath. The defeat of Goliath prepared him for leadership in King Saul's army. Dealing with a jealous king and having to run for his life for a decade prepared him to lead Israel. He dealt with many vicissitudes of survival, betrayal, victories and failures, all of which built his resume. Only after years of rather intense preparation was David ready to step into the role as king of Israel—to which he had been anointed by Samuel some ten years earlier. Clearly, David was not ready to be king the day after he was anointed to be king. However, once David was ready, the people willingly followed.

Without overemphasizing the obvious, being a leader necessitates having followers. People must be willing to submit to the leader's oversight and direction. In other words, people have to want to follow you. A forced following is a dictatorship. In a dictatorship, people follow and comply out of compulsion and fear. In many cases where dictatorships have failed, the liberated people violently turn on the dictator in an explosive release of anger and frustration to satisfy a sense of revenge.

Therefore, whenever you have a congregation that has entrusted its spiritual and, in many cases, socioeconomic and even physical wellbeing to the pastor, it is a sacred thing that is to be respected. You always have to keep in mind you are not to lord over God's people. Considering all of the churches out there, people do not have to attend the church you are pastoring. Ultimately, they are there because they want to be there, and not because they have to be there.

Once you have their trust as a pastor, it is your job to develop them by way of discipleship to be a congregation that is loyal to you as the pastor and supportive of the vision God has given you for the church. Loyal people can never be taken for granted in ministry because these are the people whom God is going to use to bring the vision to fruition and fulfillment. You need committed people.

THE BUY-IN

Why is all of this so important? It's all about the buy-in. Marketing researchers and psychologists have always known that in order to sell a product, the product must be promoted by someone the people recognize as being trustworthy, i.e., a famous movie star or athlete. This makes it easier for the people to buy in or buy the product. People may not completely understand the mechanisms or the fine details, but when they see the familiar face they trust, they will give the new product a try. Similarly, if the people have bought in to you as the pastor, buying in to the vision becomes a more palatable endeavor. And for what they don't understand, their respect for your leadership and you as the pastor will keep them on board because they trust God is using you to do what is best.

Getting people to buy in is not so much about the thing or the objective to be accomplished, but comes mainly when people buy in to you as their pastor. When people buy in to you, you will not have to put forth so much effort into selling them on something. You don't have to become a used car salesman trying to convince someone a lemon will be the best car they have ever driven. No, when people have your trust and support, they already know you have their best interest at heart. That is something that is pleasing to the Lord for the betterment of the ministry.

Once you have reached the buy-in point with the people, you still need something obtainable or winnable that you can accomplish in order to build the people's confidence. Do not take on the loftiest of projects right out of the gate. Pace yourself and tackle small, obtainable goals that can be won together. This will instill confidence in the people and you as a leader. With a few wins under your belt, you can soar to greater heights.

One of the passionate accounts of people being completely committed to their leader is when David uttered these words, "Oh that one would give me a drink of the water of the well of Bethlehem, that *is* at the gate" (see 1 Chronicles 11:17-19). David didn't order his men to risk their lives to get him a drink of water. That was not the intent of his heart. But just hearing their king's wish, some loyal soldiers, without a direct order, broke through the enemy lines and got David the water he so desired. This is loyalty. This type of loyalty only comes in the context of people who have reached the buy-in point. Their resolve was that of commitment. Today, no one is asking anyone to risk their lives, but the principle is the same. When people have bought in to you as the pastor, buying in to the vision comes much easier, and they pursue objectives with a can-do attitude. Leaders need followers and followers need leaders. A leader must master the art of leading in order for the people to buy in.

CHAPTER 12

DON'T LOSE YOUR MAP

Back before the technological revolution of the late 20th century, people who did any interstate travel throughout the United States were at the mercy of having an accurate road map. For example, if you were traveling from Chicago to Memphis, you could stop at almost any gas station and go to the map section and purchase a road map. These road maps were printed on a large piece of paper that was folded several times to a more convenient, smaller size. Once you got in your vehicle and unfolded the map, it would practically take up the space of both front seats, as you marked your destination and traced your route.

Today, paper maps are obsolete and have been replaced with global positioning satellite (GPS) technology. Now, our smartphones and state-of-the-art vehicles have interactive, computerized maps that respond to voice commands, and give turn-by-turn audio directions. We can even get a calculation of when we will arrive at our destination. Whether one uses a primitive paper map or GPS technology, the purpose of the map is to give us directions to reach our destination. Secondly, and even more importantly, a map helps prevent you from getting lost along the way.

Getting lost is a process. One wrong turn leads to another. The farther you go in the wrong direction, the deeper you get in being lost. Often, there is no accompanying feeling that you are lost. Many times you can be lost and not realize it until you end up in the wrong place. A ship out at sea can be off just one degree, and after a few days, be hundreds or even thousands of miles off course. At sea, there are no road signs or gas stations, and all the water looks the same. You can end up lost before you know it. The same is true in ministry, particularly in the area of doctrine. Here, a pastor must protect himself and the congregation against the perils of getting lost doctrinally. Therefore, pastors must, with all diligence, not lose their map.

Lead by Your Biblical and Theological Convictions

Since the beginning, there have been a plethora of doctrinal differences and controversies that have always circulated throughout the church. Varying opinions on just about any theological or ecclesiastical subject are inevitable. Historically, the councils and synods of antiquity (e.g., Nicaea, Chalcedon, Carthage and many others) were mostly convened to settle fundamental doctrinal issues. Later, doctrinal disputations even sparked a movement that would ignite the Protestant Reformation, causing a split from the Catholic and giving rise to Protestant churches of today. So there have always been and always will be debates about doctrine. However, today's pastor needs to be well informed in his doctrinal persuasions. Whether they are denominational or personal, everyone must have sound biblical convictions to which they must be anchored to or they will get off course and run aground doctrinally.

For example, if you have agreed to be part of a denominational organization, then you have also agreed to be on the same page in accordance with the fundamental doctrinal tenets of that organization. If you are a cessationist (the belief that spiritual gifts discontinued with the completion of the canon of Scripture), then why join a Pentecostal organization or pastor a Charismatic church? It is essential to stay grounded in what you believe. It is important to be secure in the fundamentals of the Christian faith and be on guard against the intrusions of false doctrine and new age philosophy and also be mindful of infusions of secular humanism creeping into your congregation and influencing uninformed members who are not seasoned enough in the Word of God to prevent imbibing heretical teaching.

The Influences of Popular Doctrinal Trends

One of the complications of being immersed in the technological age is that we're bombarded with all sorts of information and trends, many of which are bad. The question may be: How is bad doctrine so easily spread? The answer is simple: When popular preachers with a large platform give their opinions and spout their revelations, those unskilled in the Word are easily mesmerized. People grab hold of bad doctrine simply because a certain popular televangelist says so. Doctrines such as "name it claim it" and "speaking your reality into existence" are nothing more than repackaged pantheism (i.e., new age philosophy). They coincide with the teaching found in the popular book *The Secret*, spouting the "law of attraction" as a driving force behind attracting wealth and prosperity to yourself by speaking positive words. Teachings like these are enormously popular and are very attractive, especially to those with "itching ears," but they are not biblical and are antithetical to sound Christian doctrine.

For a church struggling to pay the monthly bills, it is easy to be pulled into this type of dissimulation, causing the pastor and the congregation to slowly but surely be pulled off course. This is why as a pastor, you cannot lose your map doctrinally, and you cannot lose your map personally, which means you cannot lose your identity. You cannot lose your own voice. Know who you are and what you stand for, and be able to articulate and defend that. Eventually, every pastor will have to deal with someone slithering their way into the congregation and attempting to bring in doctrine contrary to what is being taught. You must confront, reject and, if necessary, eject anyone who is contrary or brings division into your congregation. As the Bible warns, "A little yeast works through the whole batch of dough" (Gal. 5:9, NIV). In Titus, the Scriptures instruct: "Warn a divisive person once, and then warn them a second time. After that, have nothing to do with them" (Titus 3:10, NIV).

Additionally, be on guard for intrusions into your spirit, to avoid being influenced by what's popular. Yes, maintain your doctrinal map, but also maintain your personal map. Do not try to be someone you are not, or else the congregation will not know which preacher is showing up on Sunday, as you vacillate between different trendy preachers and their messages. In trying to keep up other preachers, it's easy to lose yourself. It's easy to lose your own voice. Stay with your biblical, theological and personal convictions because that helps solidify you as a person, preacher and a leader. You will never be settled in your spirit if you attempt to imitate someone else. Your church is not Saddleback or Potter's House. God has prepared you for the congregation He has called you to lead. You have to find your voice because that will be the voice your congregation is following. Never attempt to be a cheap imitation of someone else. You are the best you that God has ever created.

THE STIGMAS ABOUT MONEY

Some preachers are afraid to teach about money. Why? Because of the stigmatization attached to the "name it claim it" prosperity gospel that has proliferated in many quarters of the church. However, as pastors and teachers, we should not shy away from teaching about money just because some have placed an overemphasis on the subject. The truth is, teaching about money is a part of the whole counsel of God. We cannot claim to teach the truth but at the same time be afraid to teach about money. Pastors have the responsibility to teach how to handle finances.

At the first church I pastored, because of the money stigma, I never taught about money. Consequently, we never had much money. We were always financially struggling because I was afraid to teach about money. Since then, I have learned the whole counsel of God must be taught. The truth is the truth, and we must not be afraid of teaching the truth. Subsequently, the pastor who took over the church after I left wasn't afraid to teach about money, and the church's financial standing turned around considerably. Remember this: God has never had a problem with people, communities, businesses and churches having good success. The issue usually is how one goes about obtaining it and the position wealth occupies in one's heart. You cannot serve God and wealth. However, if you seek the Kingdom of God and its righteousness, the things will be added to you. Trust me—God knows how to add.

Positions and Persuasions Can Change

Certainly, there are fundamentals that should never be compromised. For example, there is no room for change when it comes to the atoning sacrifice and death of Jesus Christ and His resurrection from the dead. However, we may have various views on eschatology as it relates to the rapture of the church, whether one is pre, mid, pre-wrath or post-trib. These theories are all debatable. There is no need to fall out or disfellowship someone over these issues. Another debate is whether women should be in the clergy. You might change positions on that or switch from pre-trib to post-trib; these are secondary issues that fall in the realm of the debatable. In Romans, the apostle Paul categorized debatable issues as *doubtful disputations* (disputable matters, NIV), and admonished the church to let love prevail and be charitable to others' persuasions that might be different than yours, but not heretical or destructive.

Guard against accepting something just because the pastor down the street believes it or practices it. Stick to your own core beliefs and convictions. Do not give in to something just because it is contemporary, or because everyone else is doing it. We tell our children this all the time. So what if your friend is coloring their hair green? That does not mean you're supposed to do it. The same is true in ministry. Learn to be successful with who you are. You cannot be successful building on another man's foundation. You are unique. God has specially gifted you for what He has called you to do. You are God's workmanship created in Christ Jesus ordained to good works, that we should walk in them. This is why as you are going forth in your ministerial journey, you cannot afford to lose your map.

CHAPTER 13

KNOW YOUR BUSINESS

After four hundred years as slaves in Egypt and the long-awaited Exodus had finally come, Moses found himself at a critical point in his leadership. With Pharaoh's army swiftly approaching from the rear, surrounded by hostile wilderness, and the Red Sea before them, Moses had little time to make a crucial decision. There was no time to poll the elders, ask the people's opinion, or take a vote on whether they should surrender and go back to bondage, stand and fight against an over-whelming superior army, or go forward into the Red Sea. Well, enough of us have read this account in the Scriptures or at least have seen the Cecil B. DeMille classic *The Ten Commandments* to know how this story ends. Miraculously, God opens up the Red Sea, Israel goes forward and escapes, while Pharaoh's army drowns as the Red Sea collapses upon them. However, had Moses listened to the people, they would not have gone back to Egypt as slaves. No, by that time Pharaoh had already taken that option off the table. They would have been slaughtered.

As any experienced leader will tell you, a crisis requiring critical decision-making, does not wait until the most opportune or convenient time to pop up. However, what will be a great determining factor in the outcome of such a crisis is how well you know your business.

I have often heard it said there are two sides to the church, consisting of a business side and spiritual side. However, I need everyone reading this book to understand that statement is incorrect. There is only one side of a church. How is it I can make that claim? It is simple. God is spiritual, and everything He does is about His glory. It is true there are many aspects of a church, but they all fall under "as unto the Lord." It's all about God, and everything done in or through the church should be for His glory. At the end of the day, if whatever a church is doing is not about the glory of God, you are wasting your time. You might as well pack up, shut the doors of the church and go home. Everything a church does should be about God's glory, even when it comes to how we manage the church's money.

Ask yourself: If it's not about honoring God, then why are we doing it? If the church walks away from its primary purpose of honoring God, it's heading in the wrong direction. Going back to the Exodus, how would God have been honored if His people had been slaughtered by Pharaoh? How would God have been honored by Israel going back into the bondage from which they had just been delivered? There is no honor in that. The only way God is honored is by Him showing his mighty power in the defeat of Pharaoh's army, in which that account preceded Israel and brought fear to Israel's enemies as they heard about the power of Israel's God. So even in the context of crisis, there is the opportunity to concentrate and consecrate honor to God. Compartmentalizing the business side from the spiritual side can cause you to make the wrong decision because it is easy to invite God's presence in the sanctuary but close Him out of the boardroom.

GOD AND MONEY

One of the most striking passages of Scripture concerning God and money is found in Matthew 6:24: "No one can serve two masters. Either you will hate the one and love the other, or you will be devoted to the one and despise the other. You cannot serve both God and money" (wealth, NASB). The phrase "no one" cannot be overlooked. No one means that there isn't a person on earth who can successfully serve money and God at the same time. Between the two of these, one is going to take the backseat. That's simply the way it is. However, let's delve a little further into this money matter.

In Deuteronomy 8:17-18, hear what the Lord says to Israel: "You may say to yourself, 'My power and the strength of my hands have produced this wealth for me.' But remember the LORD your God, for it is he who gives you the ability to produce wealth, and so confirms his covenant, which he swore to your ancestors, as it is today." Here, God points out two very important things: 1) If you have wealth, He gave you the power or ability to get it. 2) God gives wealth to confirm His covenant. In other words, the fact God provides the wealth is a confirmation to His covenant, in short, meaning it's for His glory.

All wealth comes from God, because it all belongs to Him anyway. All the silver and gold and the cattle on a thousand hills belong to Him. This is why God cannot be removed from the money or business side of the equation. And this is why the concept of there being a spiritual and business side of the church is wrong. All of it has to be about honoring God. Compartmentalizing leads to compromising. That's the mistake so many pastors make. They end up piercing themselves through with so many sorrows because they want to isolate the business side while they compartmentalize God out. Whenever God is not the center in all matters concerning the church, priorities get skewed and wrong decisions, especially financial ones, are made.

It's important to understand the church has business affairs to manage, but there is no separate business side to the church. Know your business. You are not the pastor to become an entrepreneur, become famous, or have the biggest church on the block. Your business as a pastor is to make disciples of Christ. Now, in the process of making disciples, the Lord for his own glory may bless you with secondary things, but your primary business is to use your God-given gifts and resources to make disciples for His glory.

MANAGING MONEY MATTERS

Having emphasized the fact there is not a separate business side of the church, I am in no way minimizing the importance of fiduciary responsibility and competence in managing money. Churches inherently raise money as tax-exempt charitable organizations. Due to this, churches have the responsibility to ensure they are in compliance with state and federal regulations concerning how funds are handled.

A situation with a pastor arose where the pastor was receiving cash from the Sunday offerings. Somehow, investigators from the IRS got wind of these transactions. Not only was the pastor charged with tax evasion, but also embezzlement of church funds. Even though he was given the money off the books, since he didn't claim it as income, it became tax evasion. Secondly, since it was off the books and not claimed as income, it is as if he was taking church money for his personal use; therefore, embezzlement. The pastor was sentenced to 18 months in federal prison for mismanaging money matters.

Another pastor once stated that in the twenty-plus years he was pastor, he only attended one or two church business meetings. He let the financial types handle the business aspect, while he handled the spiritual aspect. The reason for this was the pastor didn't understand business. Therefore, he let the people who had more expertise have financial control, which meant the CPA and MBA controlled the direction of the church, not the pastor. As for the pastor, he was content with just preaching on Sundays. As a result, the church made some bad financial decisions that could have been avoided had the pastor understood the principles of business. One of those decisions the board made was to get rid of the pastor.

KNOW YOUR BUSINESS

Let's turn our attention to basics. One of the things about good business practices is it doesn't make a difference how many people belong to the church or how big your budget is; the principles are the same. You simply cannot spend more than you take in and expect to prosper. It doesn't make a difference if you have five members or five thousand members. You can only do what you are financially able to do. Your church must have more coming in than you have going out, or you will never get ahead.

Pastors must avoid the temptation to mimic churches that have larger budgets and more resources. For example, a church with solid financials can afford to bring in a big speaker or have a well-known artist perform at an event. But when a church with fewer resources tries the same things, they risk running their church financially into the ground. So if something unexpected occurs, like the air conditioning or roof units need replacing, then they can't do what is necessary because they have not responsibly managed their financial resources. Knowing how to read and understand financial statements is today's church business.

Being a good preacher is great. Knowing how to exegete a Scripture is fantastic. Understanding deep theological concepts is wonderful, but the pastor's responsibility goes far beyond teaching Bible class and preaching on Sundays. The man of God has to know how to manage money and show leadership in making financial decisions concerning the church. Know your business, and be mindful of your business. If you ever pastor a church, remember you are not an entertainer. You are not a celebrity. You have been called to take care of the Father's business.

THE LEAVEN OF THE LAODICEANS

One of the greatest temptations in the area of business a pastor can fall prey to is being enticed and seduced by the "prosperity gospel." According to this doctrine, the pursuit of wealth is promoted as the primary sign of God's favor. There are numerous televangelists and churches that teach God wants every Christian to be rich. The concept behind this popular doctrine is transactional. God will pour out blessings in the form of wealth when you give tithes and sacrificial offerings to the church. This doctrine appeals to both pastor and parishioner alike who have been seduced by greed.

Though there are Scriptures that contradict this doctrine, one in particular is found in the book of Revelation, where Jesus rebukes the Laodiceans. The following is the harshest rebuke given to any of the seven churches:

> So, because you are lukewarm, and neither hot nor cold, I will spit you out of my mouth. For you say, I am rich, I have prospered, and I need nothing, not realizing that you are wretched, pitiable, poor, blind, and naked. I counsel you to buy from me gold refined by fire, so that you may be rich, and white garments so that you may clothe yourself and the shame of your nakedness may not be seen, and salve to anoint your eyes, so that you may see.
>
> Revelation 3:16-18

If there is any passage that refutes the prosperity gospel, this passage does. Clearly, the Lord verbalizes what He thinks of a rich congregation that trusts in their money and possessions—they made Him nauseous. It's one thing not to manage money properly, but it's another thing altogether to trust and be motivated by money. Those who have utilized the ministry for their personal piggy bank have pierced themselves through with many sorrows. Whenever you make it a priority to amass wealth by way of the ministry, you have lost sight of why God has called you to be a pastor. Getting rich through the ministry is not your business; it is making disciples for the glory of God.

CHAPTER 14

TRANSPARENCY, TRANSPARENCY, TRANSPARENCY, AGAIN I SAY, TRANSPARENCY

Transparency is an interesting word. By definition it means *easily seen through, recognized or detected*. So, when we say transparency within the context of ministry, what is it we are really implying? For the pastor, much of what we say and do is before the congregation, whereas other aspects of ministry are confidential and of a sensitive nature. Therefore, there are many things to consider when tackling the broad subject of transparency.

Some questions that inevitably arise when discussing transparency concern disclosure—what to disclose, when disclose, where to disclose. There are some things you can disclose publicly and others you cannot. In fact, inappropriate disclosure can cause personal and corporate liability, and you could end up in court. However, the more salient point is to avoid the pitfalls of the hidden agenda. Hidden agendas speak to concealed motives. At some point, every pastor when making a crucial decision in ministry must do so in consideration of a balanced approach between transparency or nondisclosure. However, the primary reason for this discussion will be to address the problems having a hidden agenda.

In the Gospel of John, the discourse between Jesus and Nicodemus is informative. Jesus states, "Everyone who does evil hates the light, and will not come into the light for fear that their deeds will be exposed." In regards to our discussion, what we can take away from this passage is that the whole premise of a hidden agenda is to avoid exposure. Whenever a pastor embarks on any church business endeavor, it should be governed by transparency. On the other hand, if the pastor or ministry is embarking on something clandestine and seeking to avoid exposure, chances are this endeavor is incorrect, illegal and/or immoral. You must ask yourself: If this got out, what would the consequences be? If you feel you need to hide it, then chances are you shouldn't be doing it. This is where being transparent will help you stay in bounds. There is a thin line between maintaining confidentiality and hiding something. The first is an issue of prudent discretion and the other reeks of scandal.

I have often heard it said not to say or do something to someone else you would not say to their face. If you wouldn't say it to them, then why say the same thing about them to someone else? Chances are, it will get back to that person anyway, and a big mess can start. Again, transparency here is important because it will temper what is said about someone to others. An old friend of mine who was in the navy stated there was a saying he used to hear, which was "loose lips, sink ships." Here, we have an opposite extreme to transparency; revealing too much can be equally troublesome and inappropriate.

Transparency cannot be seen as a stand-alone issue, because it needs to be propped up by discernment and discretion. You have to know how much information can be safely disclosed. You must know what to disclose and to whom it can be disclosed. You simply cannot tell everything because some people are opportunists and will run with it. This by itself can be a serious issue because it takes time to know those among you who can be sensitive and discreet with confidential information. Again, transparency is a prudent thing, but it must be regulated by discretion.

TRANSPARENCY IN BUSINESS

I once heard a person say that if he had a million dollars, he wouldn't have a problem with tithing ten percent. That sounds great, except for the fact the same person doesn't tithe on the one hundred dollars he has now. The fact is, how a person handles the little he has informs us about how he would handle a lot. The same is true when it comes to saving money. If you are not practiced at saving on a small amount of money, chances are you wouldn't save on a large amount of money either.

What about cheating? If you would fudge the numbers on your taxes or on a loan application to hedge on a favorable outcome, that means you would lie concerning other financial matters. Why? Because it is an issue of character. A cheater will cheat on their taxes or on the golf course because he is governed by the ends justifying the means, or a win-at-any-cost mentality. Cheating comes naturally to a cheater no matter the circumstances.

In a previous chapter, I dispelled the myth of there being a spiritual side and a business side to church. Every aspect of the church should be done for God's glory; therefore, there is no side where the glory of God should not take precedence. This certainly applies to business. There are so many horror stories where pastors have been fired and even jailed for corrupt business practices. However, any business dealing that would not pass the transparency test must be avoided at all costs. Shady business deals are like quicksand. Before you know it, you are in over your head.

If you are the type who wants to win no matter the cost, or the type who will cut corners or lie to achieve a desired outcome, then you have a character issue that can lead you into some serious areas of financial compromise. No matter how gifted you are in other areas of ministry, if you are financially compromised, greedy or have hidden agendas, all these will inevitably corrupt you and your congregation, and you are heading for the rocky shores of financial ruin and disgrace.

There have been many ministers who have inherited a financial mess after taking over as pastor. Some of the financial issues may be due to some power players having too much influence over financial matters. This is where a courageous spirit and direction from the Holy Spirit must come into play because confronting these issues may involve un-covering hidden agendas that have lurked beneath the surface, causing the financial illness of the ministry. If the situation is to be correct-ed, the pastor must root out the corrupt financial dealings, along with those responsible. Failing to do so will cause you to be pulled into a corrupt financial vortex.

WHO'S LEADING WHO?

Self-examination in the life of a minister is critical. You need to know your leadership style. Are you the type who insists on having all the control? Or, at the opposite extreme, are you the one who lets everyone run you, where you can't make a decision on your own, nor can you stand firm when it is required because you are always waffling? Inde-cisiveness is akin to cowardice because an indecisive person cannot stand up to opposition and would rather run from a fight. On the other hand, a person who wants all the control is dictatorial and can destroy a church by not listening to anyone else because they believe they are the only one who's right.

How one handles money exacerbates these control issues. This is why Jesus said, "Where a man's treasure is, there your heart will be also." Once a pastor invited his board members over for a "friendly" game of Monopoly. It wasn't just about playing the game, but it was actually a strategic move. Playing a game is disarming. People drop their guard, but it still gives insight into how a person deals in business. Before the dice were rolled to start the game, the battle over who wanted to be the banker was quite telling. You'd be surprised what you can learn about a person's character from a Monopoly game. Are you strategic in your purchases, or do you spend all your money on buying everything you land on?

Granted, Monopoly is just a game, but how you play the game still gives indications of what you think about business or how you handle money. By the way, the person who insisted on being the banker was open to not sticking to the rules. He would make up rules as the game progressed and was open to cutting side deals. Even though this was just a game, would you want that person to be your church's comptroller?

Lastly, be on guard against those who have one goal in mind: getting rich. On this issue, the Bible is clear: "For the love of money is a root of all kinds of evil. Some people, eager for money, have wandered from the faith and pierced themselves with many griefs" (1 Tim. 6:10, NIV). How many times have we heard of the disastrous problems pastors bring into their lives, ruining their reputation because they wanted to get rich, usually through some nefarious scheme and/or deleterious scam, bringing shame on the church? All of these types of problems can only lurk in the shadows of a hidden agenda. However, when you walk in the light of truth, transparency and wise counsel, you will not be undone by scandal.

CHAPTER 15
THERE IS NO "I" IN TEAM

There's no doubt about it, Moses was God's man. Chosen and delivered as a child. Brought up in the wisdom, knowledge and wealth of the Egyptians. Called by God as an adult and rejected by the Pharaoh. Trained by God forty years in the house of Jethro. Stepped into his role as the deliverer. Led the people out of Egypt in the Exodus. Worked many signs and wonders, some specifically designed to authenticate his leadership and relationship with God. The list goes on and on.

With this type of resume, who could challenge Moses' role and leadership? Clearly, God was with Moses, and Moses was God's man. However, in the earlier stages of Moses' ministry, there was a critical issue with his leadership, that if not corrected, would have killed him. In Exodus 18 we find this passage:

> The next day Moses sat to judge the people, and the people stood around Moses from morning till evening. When Moses' father-in-law saw all that he was doing for the people, he said, "What is this that you are doing for the people? Why do you sit alone, and all the people stand around you from morning till evening?" And Moses said to his father-in-law, "Because the people come to me to inquire of God; when they have a dispute, they come to me and I decide between one person and

another, and I make them know the statutes of God and his laws." Moses' father-in-law said to him, "What you are doing is not good. You and the people with you will certainly wear yourselves out, for the thing is too heavy for you. You are not able to do it alone.   Exodus 18:13-18

As talented and gifted as Moses was, he was on the verge of a nervous breakdown or a heart attack. Why? Because he was trying to do everything himself. As the text informs us, Moses attempted to judge over a million people's spats, debates and contentions. People stood around him from day to night bringing all of their issues and arguments. And if Moses would have continued to do so, well the book of Exodus may have been shorter, and the book of Joshua longer. But thank God for Jethro!

The question is, why did Moses feel he was the only one who could handle all the people's issues himself? And secondly, why did it take someone else to pull his coattails to confront him and say, "Son-in-law, you are about to work yourself into a coronary"?

Thirdly, surely Moses must have felt the weight of the load he was trying to carry was way too much for him, so why didn't he reach out for help on his own? Obviously, Moses had some leadership issues that caused him to think he had to do everything himself. Maybe it was his resume that stroked his ego. Maybe he was surround by people who didn't know their right hand from their left hand. Maybe it was because Moses had low self-esteem issues that caused him to need to be in control. The reasons could be endless, but the problem is Moses was behind the wheel now. He couldn't let his personal issues start clouding his leadership capabilities with over a million people's lives at stake. Even though he didn't know how to ask for help, thank God there was someone close to him to convince him he needed help.

THE JETHRO PRINCIPLE

Not a lot is known about Jethro other than he was the priest of Midian who took Moses in and introduced him to his daughters (Moses married one of them, Zipporah). However, the event that stands out most about Jethro is the wise counsel he gave Moses which was to set an infrastructure in place to handle the leadership load. Jethro declared, "You and these people who come to you will only wear yourselves out. The work is too heavy for you; you cannot handle it alone." Therefore, Jethro gave Moses some sound advice that is still important for leaders today: *Let somebody else help you.*

Here is what Jethro advised:

> You and the people with you will certainly wear yourselves out, for the thing is too heavy for you. You are not able to do it alone. Now obey my voice; I will give you advice, and God be with you! You shall represent the people before God and bring their cases to God, and you shall warn them about the statutes and the laws, and make them know the way in which they must walk and what they must do. Moreover, look for able men from all the people, men who fear God, who are trustworthy and hate a bribe, and place such men over the people as chiefs of thousands, of hundreds, of fifties, and of tens. And let them judge the people at all times. Every great matter they shall bring to you, but any small matter they shall decide themselves. So it will be easier for you, and they will bear the burden with you. If you do this, God will direct you, you will be able to endure, and all this people also will go to their place in peace.
>
> Exodus 18:18-23

Here, Jethro is introducing the leadership team concept. Lead as a team. Work together as a team. Share the load as a team. What this does is make the load lighter because they (the team) share it with you. The result of sharing the workload? "You will be able to stand the strain, and all these people will go home satisfied."

Leading as a team will result in the best outcomes for everyone. However, the biggest impediment to effective team leadership is "I". In the middle of the word *pride* is "i", and we know what the Bible says about pride: "It goes before destruction and a haughty spirit before a fall" (Prov. 16:18). This "I" factor—me, myself and I—has been the cause of many leaders' downfall. The Bible is full of accounts where prideful leadership caused the downfall of leadership and nations alike.

Pride will make a leader feel as though all of his decisions are right and everyone else is wrong. Pride does not allow for others' opinions and insights to be heard. When an endeavor is successful, pride will not share the credit or the spotlight. Pride only seeks self-glorification and will not even give God the glory. Pride thinks of self-interest before that of others and is typically self-righteous, self-congratulatory and controlling. Pride will steal others' ideas and take them as your own so you can look better than others. Pride will not allow others with gifts to function, for fear of someone else getting credit or being declared better at something. Pride does not want to share; it wants to be the only one seen. Pride is so antithetical, so contrary, so opposite to the team. Great leaders share success as a team, but they often take the responsibility for failure on themselves. They purposely avoid the blame game when something goes wrong because it is a sign of weakness to hear a leader whining about someone else's mistake. As Teddy Roosevelt would state, "The buck stops with me."

As a pastor, you must avoid the temptation of being a control freak or being an autocratic leader. You do not have all the knowledge. You do not have all the answers. You do not possess all the gifts. You need everyone in that church whom God has sent there. A local church is a functioning body of believers where each member plays an important part. It has never been the pastor's job to be everything or to do everything. The congregation is a body. The congregation and its leaders are a team. Teams have the same goal, the same objectives and the same purpose. What football player on a team wears a different uniform from others on the team? What team has players who wear different colors? You should all be uniform in what you do. The team concept fosters camaraderie and support for one another's good for the purpose of being in one accord to fulfill the common purpose for God's glory.

On occasion, you will run into a person who claims they don't have anyone capable of providing the help they need. This is merely a justification for not working as a team. However, good leaders develop other good leaders. If you become a mentor and coach for the people God has given you, you are developing a capable support system to help you in the time of need. Good leaders are strong enough to share in the success and have the fortitude to take the heat when the team gets it wrong.

Therefore, we should always lead as a team. Serve as a team. Achieve as a team. Worship as a team and, by all means, win as a team. Again, what's noticeably missing from the "team" equation is the letter "i" because there is no "i" in team.

CHAPTER 16

DON'T TAKE IT PERSONAL

Being a pastor is certainly not as easy as it looks. Those who observe the pastor from a distance see all the out-front activities but not the behind-the-scenes, day-to-day occurrences, challenges and frustrations from both internal and external sources. On Sunday, the people applaud you, but throughout the week is when you have to deal with the people's conflicts, complaints and frustrations. Many of these conflicts are directed at one another, some at the ministry as a whole, and still others are directed at you. People can turn against you on a dime—love you one minute, then run you down in the next minute.

The fickle nature of people is dramatized during what is called Jesus' triumphant entry into Jerusalem. Yes indeed, they cried out "Hosanna!" "Blessed is he who comes in the name of the Lord" (Mark 11:9, NIV). However, after all the adulation was over, these same people would later cry out, "Crucify him."

The purpose of this chapter; however, is not to determine all the causes of why people can be so easily swayed against the pastor, but to emphasize this one thing: You are never going to please all of the people all of the time. No matter what it is you are doing, or how much time you have put into doing it, or how well you are doing it, someone is not going to like it and will criticize you for it. The simple but effective advice I can give you, after pastoring over twenty years, is: "Don't take it personally." For your own mental, emotional and professional stability, again I say, Don't take it personally."

Years ago, there was a very thought-provoking episode of Rod Serling's classic series *The Twilight Zone* titled *On Thursday We Leave for Home*. I encourage you to watch this episode because it has some interesting insights concerning leadership gone wrong. In this case, a domineering individual called "the captain" was leading a group of people who had been stranded on an asteroid in outer space for thirty years. The captain directed all the people's day-to-day activities, judged all their issues, made all the work assignments, developed all the rules and executed all of the discipline. Since most of the people on the asteroid had been born on the asteroid, they knew nothing of the earth. Therefore, the captain, in sermonic fashion, would gather the people together and tell them amazing stories about planet Earth. Eventually, the long-awaited day arrived when they received word they were getting rescued. Everyone was elated, but for the captain, the problem was just beginning.

After the rescuers landed, they announced that on Thursday every-one would be leaving for home. However, immediately the captain felt threatened because he knew back on earth, the people would no longer need him as their leader. On the asteroid, they depended upon him, but on earth, they would be free to live out their lives without him. They could make all their own decisions. Therefore, the captain became so threatened and upset he tried to sabotage the trip back home. He became so opposed to the idea that the people would be liberated he made the decision not to get on the ship. He took things personally to such a degree that he made the fatal decision to live out the rest of his life alone on that asteroid. As he watched the spacecraft take off from the asteroid, he yelled out, "Wait for me, I want to go home!" Obviously, it was too late. This fictionalized sci-fi episode com-municates powerful truths for leadership in everyday life.

The question is: What's really happening when you take things per-sonally? When you take things personally, everything becomes about you—your feelings, your emotions, your rights and your vindication. As a result, you lose your objectivity and begin to see everything through the lens of your hurt emotions. When you approach opposition from others through the lens of your own hurt, the priority becomes relieving your pain, getting even and showing people who is the boss. Doing so causes you to make decisions based on what is best for you and not for the church. You must be careful not to be isolated on your own little asteroid orbiting around the wounds given to you by others.

Once again, this is something seminary cannot teach you. One of the reasons is because no one else knows what problems and oppositions you will face. There is no curriculum that will address all the people's issues and circumstances capable of splitting a church. Besides that, many of these academic types who teach in seminaries have never pastored a church. Theirs is to expound on the theoretical, historical and theological abstractions in a classroom setting. They can tell all about John Calvin and Martin Luther, but they cannot tell how to handle when Calvin and Martin in your church rise up against you. You pastor where the rubber meets the road, not from the ivory tower of academia. These are two very distinct perspectives.

When I first began pastoring, I often took things personally. I used to hear all of the horror stories about a pastor and his family having the desire to do meaningful, fulfilling work for the Lord, but ending up getting torn to pieces by ungrateful members of a congregation. On the other hand, when a church is young and there aren't many members, the nagging question is: Will they return next week? These are just some of the burdens pastors carry from day to day, week to week. No matter how excellent the service was last week, will they return this week? So you work hard preparing that dynamic Bible class or that liberating sermon, and you put all that hard work into it, long hours in study, burning the midnight oil, sacrificing time from your family, and then when people don't show up for midweek Bible class or Sunday service, it's natural to take it personally. However, the minute you do that, you open the door to frustration, heartache, disappointment and, eventually, the reluctance to lead.

Whenever a pastor crosses the threshold to becoming insensitive, it becomes an us-against-them mentality. That's not the heart a pastor should have, because that insensitivity will not only play out in the church, but will start to affect other areas of your life, in particular, your home life. Once you start operating with an us-against-them mentality, you will become critical and judgmental. That's definitely the wrong spirit. The following passage gives us an example of what having the wrong spirit will produce:

> When the days drew near for him to be taken up, he set his face to go to Jerusalem. And he sent messengers ahead of him, who went and entered a village of the Samaritans, to make preparations for him. But the people did not receive him, because his face was set toward Jerusalem. And when his disciples James and John saw it, they said, "Lord, do you want us to tell fire to come down from heaven and consume them?" But he turned and rebuked them. And they went on to another village.
>
> Luke 9:51-56

Whenever you take things personally, your natural response is to take offense or to defend yourself. Here is where your own emotions can become your worst enemy. You want to be careful about responding emotionally, because if your purpose is to save souls, you don't want to damage the person(s) you are trying to save. Here is where a pastor with the wrong spirit can by himself destroy the church. God put you there to lead. You must remember this is not *your* church and these are not *your* people. The minute you put yourself in the wrong position, you are going to get your feelings hurt. And since we are only human, still being sanctified daily ourselves, we cannot avoid or even control having our feelings hurt. However, you can control how you respond to church and people hurt. By making a concerted effort to not take things personally, you will save yourself a lot of anguish and sleepless nights. Let's face it, a lot of the problems you will face will come from people who need to go anyway.

We must be able to discern difficult people from those with difficulties. A person with difficulties will often act like a difficult person, but they are not the same. A person with difficulties is a person who has some internal issues that are causing them to act out. In these individuals, the issues usually have nothing to do with the pastor or the church.

Unfortunately, they take their frustration out on those they believe are most vulnerable.

However, a difficult person is better internally, but is being used by Satan to stop progress, regardless of how they see you, the church or the issue. With this person, it takes prayer and the grace of God to intervene. A person with difficulties will change once their personal issues are rectified. Oftentimes, getting to understand this person and their issues will change how they act.

You must always remember, people are going to make decisions the way they want to, no matter what you say to them or what you do for them. As a pastor, you have no control over that, and believe me, you don't want that much control anyway. Pastors who have too much control over people cross over into becoming cult leaders.

Another important aspect to consider about the pitfalls of taking things personally is that it can ruin your self-esteem. Whenever your self-esteem is damaged, it can cause you to feel isolated and defeated, where you begin to second-guess yourself concerning everything you do. These are symptoms of you having crossed over into emotional leadership, where you wear your feelings on your sleeve. Then, when someone does give you constructive criticism, and there will be times when you need it, you might respond inappropriately and needlessly damage a relationship. An emotionally unbalanced pastor can be a one-man wrecking ball who singlehandedly tears down the church he worked so hard to build.

It is also important to realize you cannot stop people from talking or gossiping. They will talk about you, your wife and your children. They will talk about the car you drive. If it's old, you are mismanaging your money and you don't have enough class. If the car you drive is too new or a luxury car, you must be stealing money. If your wife dresses too well, they'll say, "Who's she trying to impress?" If she dresses modestly, they'll say she lacks taste. People are going to talk. If they talked about Jesus, they'll talk about you. Don't take it personally, or you will become hateful. People are more *green* than they are *mean*. Like children, they don't have enough maturity to control their tongues.

They are not as mean as they sound, but it's because they're green or immature. In a church you have seasoned, mature members and you have babes in Christ who have some growing to do. And in the most extreme case, some people in church are not born again. They attend church religiously, but are not saved. This is why you cannot let things get under your skin.

In all of your getting, get understanding, and don't take it personally.

CHAPTER 17

WATCH OUT FOR POTHOLES

One of the phenomena that are particular to areas of the country that experience winter months is the pothole. Potholes appear on streets and expressways and occur because of the chemical reaction between deicing elements such as salt and the asphalt, in combination with temperature fluctuations and the stress of traffic. These potholes can be big. If you hit one, it can flatten your tire and also cause serious front-end damage. When you see a pothole, you can avoid it. The problem is that you don't always see them soon enough to avoid them. Some years ago, this actually happened to me while driving on Chicago's Dan Ryan expressway, where I hit a big pothole. I couldn't avoid it, and it burst my tire, crippling my vehicle immediately. I was forced to change my tire on a busy and quite dangerous expressway.

My experience with the dreaded pothole serves as a metaphor for the potholes that you can run into while serving in the ministry. In this case, potholes can be anything that you can fall into along the way that causes damage to you or the ministry. You must be on guard against potholes and be careful to avoid them. It is important to understand that a pothole that is avoided poses no threat. But if you hit one, it's going to cause some unwanted problems.

In chapter 3, I covered the importance of a pastor being selfish, which means, take time out for yourself. It is so easy to get caught up in the myriad of duties that a pastor must face in discharging spiritual leadership in God's church. There are forces outward and inward that will quickly distract you and cause you to drift off course, especially the ones that involve a moral lapse.

No matter how saved you think you are, what title you carry or what degree you have earned, by nature, human beings are sinners. Now, I do understand that positionally we are the righteousness of God in Christ, and have been declared righteous by the atoning work of Christ, but let us not get it confused, you are not righteous through your own efforts. We must be vigilant that we live a life worthy of Him who called us into the ministry. Paul puts it this way:

> Every athlete exercises self-control in all things. They do it to receive a perishable wreath, but we an imperishable. So I do not run aimlessly; I do not box as one beating the air. But I discipline my body and keep it under control, lest after preaching to others I myself should be disqualified.
>
> 1 Corinthians 9:25-27

The games Paul is referring to are where we get our Olympic Games of today. Paul notes that those who are competing at that level must go through some rigorous training in order to compete and win the prize. This training is with great intentionality and not aimless. Not being aimless means being focused on winning and defeating the opponent, which in our case is the devil. This is where being selfish plays a major role, because you have to take time out for yourself to train spiritually because of the fight that we are in, against the strategies of the devil. Failing to do so will cause you to hit a pothole, where you will end up falling into sin.

The writer of Hebrews chimes in on this subject when he writes:

> Therefore, since we are surrounded by so great a cloud of witnesses, let us also lay aside every weight, and sin which clings so closely, and let us run with endurance the race that

is set before us, looking to Jesus, the founder and perfecter of our faith, who for the joy that was set before him endured the cross, despising the shame, and is seated at the right hand of the throne of God.

Hebrews 12:1-2

I must admit that I am using Scriptures in this chapter because many pastors do not read the Bible in a personal devotion manner, but only to gather sermon or teaching materials. But as Jesus stated, "You are clean through the words that I speak to you" (John 15:3). Therefore, a pastor must take time out every day to draw close to Jesus so that He will draw closer to you. Fasting and praying are another way to build up yourself so that you will be able to withstand the attacks of the devil.

A pastor's job is to train people to be effective Christians and witnesses for Jesus, which makes you a high-value target for the enemy. Satan would love to take you down over some moral lapse, whether it be adultery, fornication, pornography, greed, lying, lust, spousal abuse, or substance abuse. Problems like these can easily entangle pastors and ministers who are not taking their calling and this fight seriously. So what if you can preach the house down, and have an exhaustive knowledge of the Bible and theology, but you have hit a pothole and fallen out of fellowship with the Lord? Your gifts cannot keep you, nor will they save you when you hit a pothole. At that point the question will be not if you will suffer damage and loss, but how much damage and loss will there be.

FILL THOSE POTHOLES

Many pastors who have lost everything after hitting a pothole will tell you that they felt they were still all right with God. They were still preaching and teaching well. God didn't strike them down, so they assumed that they must still be in good standing. This is what the Bible calls the deceitfulness of sin. Sin makes you think that what you are doing is not so bad, and that no one else knows about your wrongdoing. But even worse, that God is okay with it. However, it is important that we do not get confused about the difference between the Lord giving us space to repent and there not being consequences for our actions. Remember, the pastor is a high-value target. If Satan can get you to fall, he knows that others who respect and look up to you could be damaged and maybe even fall into sin themselves in the process.

Even after being delivered from a fault, it is possible to fall back into sin. Therefore, you must be careful to not only avoid potholes, but you have to fill them up. In other words, you need to close the door to the opportunity to sin by not giving occasion to fulfill the lust of the flesh. The late, great Billy Graham was said to never travel alone, nor would he enter a hotel room without having an aid check it out before he entered. By closing the door to sin, you eliminate the opportunity. Another thing we must do is not to put confidence in our flesh. Sometimes pastors and ministers feel that they have all the bases covered. But no matter how experienced we think we are, we all have weaknesses.

So how do you fill spiritual potholes? It involves being proactive in your walk and relationship with Christ. Earlier, I covered the importance of a pastor spending quality time in studying the Word. Second, we must have an active and substantive prayer life that should be a daily activity. When I say pray, I do not mean a popcorn prayer, but a fervent time of praying, intercession and seeking God's face for help, strength and guidance. Third, have personal devotion each day with the Lord, preferably in the morning before you start your day. Like the Psalmist said, "Early will I seek you" (Ps. 63:1).

Devotion includes prayer, but it's distinct in that it's more centered around worshipping in God's presence, giving glory, honor and adoration to the Lord. Loving Him, just because He's God, with no human agenda attached. Coming before His presence with thanksgiving and entering His court with praise. The good thing about devotion is that it can occur throughout the day; whenever you think about the goodness of Jesus, give praise to God.

Fourth, get enough rest and take care of your business at home. Your wife and your children need tending to. If you neglect your home life, you are giving Satan an advantage to cause disruption in your life. Infidelity and kids gone wild are the direct result of not tending to your business-at-home issues. Of course, there are exceptions to this, but in general, the situation getting out of hand at home happens because of the pastor being too heavily involved in church and not at home. Fifth, have a system of accountability, and make yourself accountable to someone whom you can trust, who is not impressed by you. If they are impressed with who you are, they will have a difficult time being objective and may not tell you the truth when you need to hear it. Sixth, get counseling when necessary. Just because you are a pastor and give counsel to others does not mean you are not in need of counseling yourself. Being a seminary graduate and being ordained does not make you immune to falling. You cannot embrace fire and not be burned. You cannot jump into water and not get wet. The Bible warns, "Take heed lest ye fall" (1 Corinthians 10:12).

And finally, if you fall into sin, you are not alone. The Bible promises:

> No temptation has overtaken you that is not common to man. God is faithful, and he will not let you be tempted beyond your ability, but with the temptation he will also provide the way of escape, that you may be able to endure it.
> 1 Corinthians 10:13

Often when a pastor hits a pothole, he feels alone, as if no one has gone through what he is experiencing. This is exactly how sin works on a person's mind through pride, as if you are someone extraordinary dealing with something unique. Nonsense. There is no temptation that a person can encounter that is not already common to humankind, but regardless, God will provide a way of escape. The best way to escape is to watch out for the potholes.

CHAPTER 18

DEVELOP THE BEST YOU

Today, we think of the Apostle Paul as a prolific, dynamic, apostolic powerhouse. However, many of his contemporaries thought of him quite differently. The following two passages give us a glimpse into how others saw Paul, and what they thought of him and his controversial ministry.

> For they say, "His letters are weighty and strong, but his bodily presence is weak, and his speech of no account." Let such a person understand that what we say by letter when absent, we do when present. Not that we dare to classify or compare ourselves with some of those who are commending themselves. But when they measure themselves by one another and compare themselves with one another, they are without understanding. But we will not boast beyond limits, but will boast only with regard to the area of influence God assigned to us, to reach even to you.
>
> 2 Corinthians 10:10-13

Secondly,

> Indeed, I consider that I am not in the least inferior to these super-apostles. Even if I am unskilled in speaking, I am not so in knowledge; indeed, in every way we have made this plain to you in all things.
>
> 2 Corinthians 11:5-6

In the first passage, the way Paul responds to criticism is informative. Here he does not engage in name-calling or resort to pejorative terms, but he sets the record straight by saying, "What we are in our letters when we are absent, we will be in our actions when we are present." Paul was aware that he had critics. However, Paul immediately recognized the folly of those among his critics who measured, compared and commended themselves by and among themselves. This type of circular congratulatory comparison and commendation amounted to foolishness, which Paul accurately categorized as being unwise. It is unwise, because comparing yourself to someone else misses the point that we are all different and gifted in a unique way, according to the purpose and calling of God.

In the second passage, once again Paul addresses the so-called "super-apostles" who criticized Paul's lack of oratorical training. Paul's response was to state that he was in no way inferior to these super-apostles. What he lacked in rhetorical skill he made up for in knowledge, because he had been taught by a series of revelations that he had received from Christ. It was these same revelations that came down to us as 13 New Testament epistles, all attributed to Paul. Who these super-apostles were is unknown, and rightly so. Christ Himself vindicated Paul, his apostleship and his letters, and over two thousand years later, we are still reading Paul's words. That within itself is *super* vindication.

So, what can we learn from this? As ministers of God, we should work in the calling in which we were called. We should not fall into the trap of comparing ourselves to someone else. Nor should we attempt to *cop someone else's style.* It is a waste of time to try to become someone that you are not. Think about it. You are unique. No one beat you at being you. So why not develop the best you?

There are different types of criticism. There is cynical criticism, where people are simply trying to run you down because they are jealous of you or don't like you. This criticism is not designed to help, but to discourage you. If you let this criticism take root in your spirit, you will never make it in the ministry and soon give up. You need a healthy sense of self-esteem to let what the detractors are saying simply roll off you. It's not worth the time or energy to respond to this type of worthless criticism.

The other type of criticism is constructive criticism. This type of criticism is designed to help you improve. This is necessary to help us grow and develop. We see this example when Aquila and Priscilla made the acquaintance of an eloquent man named Apollos, who was mighty in the Scriptures. Acts 18:25 tells us that he "had been instructed in the way of the Lord, and he spoke with great fervor and taught about Jesus accurately, though he knew only the baptism of John." In the following verse we are told that "Priscilla and Aquila heard him, they invited him to their home and explained to him the way of God more adequately." This is a perfect example of letting someone give you constructive criticism concerning your gifts and talents so that you can develop into a better you.

What if Apollos would have had some hang-ups about someone suggesting that he tighten up Jesus' presentation? The fact is that there was more to the story that he wasn't telling. Doesn't it make sense that if you are going to do something, you should invest in yourself to make sure that you are doing it right, and to the best of your ability? In order for that to happen, you cannot be too thin-skinned to allow someone to critique you for the purpose of improving your skills and expertise. I know you may have just graduated from the top seminary in the country, but even with all that, you still do not know everything. We should be ever-learning and developing our knowledge of the truth.

Don't be ashamed of not knowing something, or saying that you don't know. How often have we been asked a question, such as, "Have you heard of this thing or that, or have you read this or that book?" Instead of being honest and saying, "No, I haven't," we say, "Yeah, I think so." Why? Because we don't want to sound as if we don't know something that we should know. We don't want to come off as being less than, so we lie. However, this is the place where honesty could be very beneficial. Maybe the person who asked you about that book would have given you a copy so you would know.

Therefore, don't be ashamed of not knowing something. Be honest and transparent enough to receive the help that will lead you to fuller development. Besides, we are all still learning, which could cause you to evolve. Maybe the way you have looked at something over the years has evolved into a greater understanding that changes the way you handle a certain topic or situation. All change is not bad. What is bad is not being big enough to make changes or to receive constructive criticism when we need it. Individuals, who are not teachable, make bad leaders. No one person possess all the gifts and all the knowledge.

Let those who are more experienced help develop you. You have absolutely nothing to lose and everything to gain, because there isn't another person in the world who can beat you at being you. You may as well invest as much time as possible in developing the best you. Stretch yourself, grow, and evolve. By doing so, you will maximize your gifts and talents.

CHAPTER 19

NAVIGATING THROUGH A CHURCH FIGHT

One of the most profound circumstances that a pastor will ever face, and a subject not found on a seminary syllabus, is how to navigate through a church fight. A church fight can be a pastor killer, both literally and figuratively. As a point of clarity, I am not speaking of a physical confrontation breaking out between people, though those do happen. I'm speaking of power players at odds over a certain contentious issue. In the more extreme cases, these contentions have split and even destroyed entire churches, and are among some of the most stressful situations that any pastor and congregation can experience. In this chapter, it is not so much the extreme circumstances that end the life of a church. I'll spend time focusing on the church fights that occur among key members of the congregation. These smaller—but not any less intense—fights that if left unchecked have the potential to ruin a church. A church divided against itself cannot continue to stand.

There are two words in this chapter title that I feel give a glimpse of hope: *navigating* and *through*. The word *navigating* brings to mind the skill and knowledge someone has to have to safely traverse an arduous or dangerous place. It's like going on a whitewater rapids tour, where you need an experienced guide to get you through this exhilarating yet potentially dangerous excursion. Though it is a bumpy, rough ride, you can get through it. That's the whole point; you can make it through a nasty church fight. What I will endeavor to do is to give you some pointers on how to come through a church fight on the winning side.

The Power Players and the Issues

In every contention there are at least two power players. However, the pastor must not be swayed by either side; his job is to navigate, to get everybody through the situation as safely as possible. In order to accomplish that, the power players on both sides need to be identified. Sometimes this is obvious, other times they must be uncovered. Some power players want to be out front; others like to remain behind the scenes and contend through proxies. In either case, it is important to understand that in any conflictual situation you must identify and bring to the table the leaders on both sides. In mediating Mideast peace treaties, you can never negotiate a ceasefire until you bring the heads to the table, where they can air out their complaints and give their list of demands so that their issues can be addressed. Even in a legal situation where two parties agree to arbitration, the arbitrator, usually a judge, hears both sides, and a workable plan and agreement is established.

The next step is getting the facts straight. What are the real issues? Often, people can be arguing over perceptions and feelings, but not facts. People often contend over what they think is right, or what they think was said, or what they assume occurred. Then issues can be compounded and convoluted to such a degree that people cannot even remember what actually started the feud in the first place. Therefore, it is necessary to discover what concerns are the main or important issues. At this point, trivial issues should be discarded or put on the back burner.

Once the *main* issues are identified, they must be put in the right context. In doing so, ask how long these issues have been going on. For example, what if a conflict was started by a person who is no longer a member of the church, but the issue has maintained momentum after their departure? Once the truth is known as to how long an issue has been a problem, we might be able to trace it back to its source. What you uncover may help both sides in understanding the need to move on from an issue that should have been dead long ago.

There are also situations where the fight is about you, the pastor.

Those conflicts are just as bad or worse. Opposition frequently rises against leadership from power players in the church, which could include deacons, ministers, administrators or influence-wielding lay people. Church fights that are directed at the pastor—and those that support the pastor—can lead to serious legal battles and court fights. In circumstances like these, it is important that you garner as much support as possible among individuals who are loyal to you. You might also consider securing legal advice from a competent attorney who specializes in church affairs.

It is important to consider the dynamics of how conflicts develop. The stated issue(s) are rarely the real bone of contention. It's the underlying issues that are usually causing the tension. Therefore, before you can navigate through a church fight, you must uncover the problems lurking beneath the surface, or the issues will never be solved. The commonality in most conflicts revolves around the three P's: power, pride and possessions.

Sometimes you have individuals in the church who like to keep disruptions going. These types of people are carnal, so the enemy uses them to continue the chaos. This is why Paul called out those who "cause divisions" (Rom. 16:17). In Proverbs, among the seven things that the Lord hates, last on the list is the one about sowing discord or conflict (Proverbs 6:16-19). Therefore, the pastor must understand that the devil is behind these disruptions. So, instead of getting in the flesh with them, you must maintain the high ground and be led by the spirit. Here is where a discerning heart is key.

Another important aspect of problem solving regarding this issue is understanding some of the pains and feelings attached to the conflict. It could be as simple as someone unintentionally getting their feelings hurt, and not letting go. So often, we do not go to those who offend us, but let things fester until they become a problem. It is important that everyone be heard. In many cases people feel as though no one is listening. Giving everyone an opportunity to voice their concerns will allow resolution to take place. Whenever people are arguing, neither side is listening.

In conflictual situations, people are often driven by fear. The fear of losing control or power is a major concern. People afraid of losing control tend to respond out of fear, and can resort to poor decision making in an effort to maintain control. Therefore, assessing and addressing someone's fears, especially the irrational ones, will go a long way in resolving conflict.

After determining who the power players are, you also need to know which groups are involved. Power players come with supporters, which help keep up the tension in the dispute. Often these are called cliques, a group of like-minded or common-issue individuals following the lead of another. Cliques—or as they are called in Galatians *factions*—can be very dangerous to the health and wellbeing of a church. Power players could be two departments within the church that are at odds: the deacon board against the ushers, or a conflict among the ministers. A conflicting issue could be a doctrinal fight or an issue over a church tradition or rule. It could be a church planning issue: Do we build a youth wing or senior citizen's development? There is a plethora of possibilities concerning conflicting issues and interests that can ignite church conflicts.

STANDING UP TO YOUR GIANTS

After you peel away all the layers of the onion, you will get to the core of the conflict, which is power. Whether it's about gaining, keeping or controlling, power is the coveted issue that no one wants to share. Power struggles can be the ugliest fights that involve lawyers and the courts, and when things get too heated, even the police. There have been many pastors locked out of their church, evicted from a parsonage, and even sued by the church. Sometimes it's the pastor's fault, and other times someone wants the pastor out because he is changing direction or attempting to reorganize, and a power player doesn't like it.

In cases like these, the pastor must stand up to those giants and not retreat. Sometimes it's worth the fight, especially when you are standing up for what's right. The question is, do you have the stamina for a protracted court or legal battle? Can you handle all the pressure and distractions from antagonists who want to see you go? Because if you can stand up to those giants and fight the good fight of faith, you and the church can come out so much better. Remember, we wrestle not against flesh and blood…but spiritual wickedness in high places.

One of the important things to remember is that people resist change. If you're coming in and instituting church reform, expect some opposition. People do not change easily, especially when it is their stake in the church that is in the crosshairs of your reform. Remember, most conflicts are about power. However, don't be afraid of conflict either. Even if it means retaining counsel and going to court. Stick it out, because the church could be so much better after the fight. The church will run much smoother after the hell raisers are gone. Not everyone in the church is born again. The tares are mixed in with the wheat. Therefore, you must remain resolute and unwavering when standing up against oppositional forces. I am not advocating for a fight, however, you cannot be afraid of a fight either. If it is the Lord's will, he will strengthen and see you through.

Rally your support. If the Lord has sent you to that church, He has prepared someone whom you can trust for backing and encouragement. Sometimes you would be surprised as to who sticks with you and who doesn't. The important thing is to stay focused, and don't take it personally. If you are making decisions based on your hurt feelings or emotions, you often make missteps and play right into the opposition's hand. Every David needs a Jonathan to give needed assistance in the time of crisis. It is often in the heat of battle that you will see who is really on your side. Never forget those who back you, because if they stick their necks out for you, they should be acknowledged and appreciated. No leader is great by himself; it takes a team effort. When the dust has settled and it is all over, you and the church will be much better off for it.

Regardless of who wins the conflict, people are not the winners. Only God's will prevails. No one should gloat about an apparent victory: either move on, or it's time for healing and uniting.

Keep It Off the Pulpit

The final aspect concerning how to handle a church fight is to never take it to the pulpit. During my first five years at Piney Grove Baptist Church, I called them the fighting years. It was an internal fight. There was the daily undermining of me. There were those who were talking about me, the phone calls, the gossip. There was the group over here and the group over there keeping up the mess. There was the disrespect, the whole nine yards. People are always amazed when I tell them that, because they were not aware that any fighting was going on. The reason for that is, I never took it to the pulpit. I never preached about my frustration in having to fight. It was internal, and I kept it that way.

The bottom line is that people do not come to church to hear about a mess. If you are airing out the church's dirty laundry over the pulpit, you will lose good people. Ironically, the messy people won't leave when you preach about their mess, just the good ones. So a pastor must consider what to say and what not to say over the pulpit. The main reason a controversy spreads is because people keep it alive by talking about it. The pulpit is for the Gospel, and not gossip. Therefore, you should not use the pulpit to beat over the head people who oppose you. It takes a bigger man to keep silent about church fights and not give in to the temptation to weaponize the pulpit. If you do so, you can make a person a martyr and put sympathy right back in their hand. Therefore, never make a person a martyr. If need be, you become the martyr.

Not All Conflict Is Bad

In his book titled *What's Love Got To Do With It*, Frank Anthony Thomas writes about the *creative clarity of conflict*, where he emphasizes that not all conflict is bad. That oftentimes there is a fusion of opposing ideals (an ultimate object or goal of endeavor) that produces even better ideas. Surely it is natural to become defensive when people oppose us. Opposition is not the desired response we want from others. However, what often happens after navigating through a conflict and opposition is that it can produce better ideas and results that benefit those involved. Therefore, it is our responsibility to examine our motives, as we attempt to understand the guiding principles of those who oppose us.

Chapter 20

You Are Not A Machine

One of the great advances in industry has been in the area of robotics. On many assembly lines, robots have replaced humans, particularly in jobs that are repetitious, and require speed and accuracy. Robots or machines in general accomplish tasks much better than people, because they are more precise and can perform functions that are beyond a person's physical ability. Therefore, manufacturers have opted to invest billions of dollars in machinery and robotic technology to keep up with commercial and industrial shifts, consumer demands and their competitors.

Machines are great, because they can work quicker, more accurately, deliver more output to a higher degree of quality than a person. They don't need coffee breaks, vacation time, health benefits or weekends off. Nor do they call in sick, need maternity leave, require raises, quit or organize unions and go on strike. For these reasons alone, many manufacturers opt for mechanized and robotic labor.

Machines are valuable because they do not require all the emotional support that people do. People have not only emotional and mental problems, but spiritual ones as well. Humans have spirits and souls to maintain. Machines do not. Humans are in need of redemption, salvation and guidance from an eternal all-knowing, ever-present and all-powerful merciful God. Machines do not. Of all these differences, there is one small feature that a machine has that humans, often to their detriment, do not have. Machines have an off switch; humans do not. That's exactly the point, particularly concerning the pastor.

You are not a machine. There is no off switch. Therefore, you must maintain yourself and build up your most holy faith or, like a machine, you will experience a breakdown. You must incorporate emotional and spiritual triage, where you are constantly assessing and evaluating your needs, as a critical part of being able to maintain stability and stamina in the ministry to avoid breakdown and burnout.

As a pastor you cannot take on too much. You cannot be in every place at every time. You cannot be all things to all people, and you are certainly not God. Though many of your functions are repetitious, you must guard against becoming apathetic and performing your duties in a perfunctory, dry, emotionless, mechanical manor. You must recognize the signs of overload and burnout, and if you see the signs of overload, head to the emergency room immediately. It's time to get yourself some help.

Pastors, like medical doctors, often make the worst patients. Since it is their job to take charge and care for others, they often do not know how to be the recipients of care. Call it ego, or call it pride. Whatever you call it, the point is that being obstinate can be a killer physically, emotionally and in ministry. Who benefits from a broken machine? Who benefits from a broken pastor, whom people depend on and look to for spiritual leadership and guidance? You're not a machine. You cannot run all day and all night, and not have it negatively affect your life. Before you know it, you will end up in the emergency room or worse.

Signs of Pastoral Burnout

Everyone in church leadership is subject to burnout. Burnout is defined as *exhaustion of physical or emotional strength or motivation usually as a result of prolonged stress or frustration.* On the basis of the definition alone, you can understand why so many ministry workers, especially the pastor, experience burnout.

Some of the signs of burnout are the constant feeling of being worn out, and lacking the energy or drive to carry out your functions. When you get up in the morning, are you dreading going to the church, or are you lacking enthusiasm? Have you lost the excitement about serving God's people? Is there dryness in your teaching or sermonic delivery? Do you feel lonely or isolated, or have you stopped caring about important things, being more apt to just let things slide? Have you let your spiritual guard down, praying less and giving in to sinful desires? Are you more irritable and easily agitated and frustrated? Have your spouse, children, associates or co-workers noticed a change in your personality? Are you getting enough rest? Are you experiencing restless nights where you do not get enough sleep? If you answered yes to these questions, you are probably experiencing—or well on your way to experiencing—burnout.

Leadership Resources.org lists four types of burnout: physical, relational, emotional and spiritual.[7]

Physical burnout is triggered by the lack of exercise. The business of ministry and multitasking required by today's pastors is overwhelming. When we are too busy, it leads to not eating healthy and not getting enough rest. If not corrected, physical burnout can lead to a compromised immune system, which opens the door to a plethora of physical maladies and illnesses. When you aren't taking care of yourself properly, you can experience physical burnout.

Relational burnout is similar to emotional burnout and can be caused by tension experienced with other church leaders and congregants. The constant daily interactions with high-maintenance individuals can drain your emotions and make you become indifferent, apathetic and short-fused. These are all symptoms of being at your wits' end, and can cause you to recoil from the very ones who need help the most. All interpersonal relationships suffer when a person is suffering from relational burnout.

Emotional burnout involves the numbness of a person's feelings. When we are numb to those around us, we cannot respond in an emotionally appropriate manner. Typically, emotional burnout causes self-doubt and low self-esteem, which greatly diminishes confidence. When we do not have confidence, we often second-guess ourselves and have difficulty being assertive, because we lack balance and the necessary self-assurance. Those experiencing emotional burnout take these issues home, where they are often misinterpreted as divided attention, which can lead to suspicion and wreak havoc in a marital relationship.

Spiritual burnout is felt when pastors fall susceptible to pouring into others' lives, while no one is pouring into theirs, and they experience being spiritually drained. Whenever a pastor is spiritually drained, they are not seeking God's face or His presence, but are typically running on "E" trying to make it through the day. Though they are in need of a fresh anointing and a spiritual revival, they attempt to survive on head knowledge as opposed to being spirit-filled. When you don't want to read the Word or cry out to God in prayer, chances are you are experiencing spiritual burnout. At that point you are most vulnerable to spiritual attacks from the enemy which lead to compromise and sin.

Therefore, you have to consider all of these areas and take care of yourself to avoid a trip to the emergency room or the morgue. Listen to the warning signs in your body, your mind and your spirit. Get spiritual triage, evaluate, and examine yourself. Get counseling, get advice, share your burdens, and be accountable to someone else. Remember, you are not a machine, and you do not have an off switch, but you can break down, and you can burn out.

The reality about burnout is far from a myth. It is a dangerous plague that often infiltrates the lives of ministers. That is the reason why so many end up leaving the ministry: they have reached the level of burnout but didn't realize it before it was too late. Burnout hinders their physical and emotional wellbeing, and even depletes their spiritual stamina.

HERE'S WHAT YOU SHOULD DO

If you have reached a point where you are tired of doing ministry, you have reached burnout. If you reached the point where you become frustrated with preparing sermons, or that you have to visit someone, or counsel with someone, you are probably at burnout. What I recommend is: 1) Go immediately into a spiritual triage mode where you are constantly assessing and evaluating your needs and identify problem areas.

2) Take time off. This is not about ministry, but about your relationship with God. This is where the minister must save himself. If you are not regularly planning to refuel, it is wise not to wait until you are on empty to take a vacation. Whether it's once a month, or once a quarter, regardless of how busy you are, you must plan time off as you would plan any other dates. It is wise to schedule spiritual retreats and get away in order to refuel and recharge. If you do not actually schedule this in, you will not keep that appointment.

3) Get away and spend time with God. In the Scriptures Jesus would often withdraw from the people and His disciples to get alone with the Father, to take a respite, a time of relief, in order to renew and regenerate. Now ask yourself, if Jesus had to get away for self-maintenance purposes, and He was the Lord of Glory, then how much more time should you take off? Even in creation, the almighty, inexhaustible, all powerful God rested on the seventh day, and sanctified the Sabbath as a day of rest, that we should observe taking time off that's dedicated to rest and renewal.

CHAPTER 21

STAY ON FIRE, STAY ON PURPOSE

But I have this against you, that you have abandoned the love you had at first.
Remember therefore from where you have fallen; repent, and do the works
you did at first. If not, I will come to you and remove
your lampstand from its place, unless you repent.
Revelation 2:4-5

Let's face it, there are times in ministry where the newness wears off, where things can become ordinary, mundane and even outright boring. The same Sunday routine, the same Easter and Christmas program, the same Sunday school lessons, the same Sunday morning hymns, the same food drives, the same summer programs, the same problems among the staff. No matter where you look in the ministry, all you see is repetition and sameness. Now the ministry you were once excited and exhilarated about has now become rigmarole, regular and routine. The question is, what has changed? Obviously it's not the ministry. To get to the truth of the matter, you don't have to look further than the mirror. Maybe the biggest contributor to the problem is you, and it might be because you have lost your fire.

In Revelation, the Lord rebukes the church at Ephesus for losing their first love. I don't think it would be beyond reason to suppose that an aspect of their problem was that the fire and fervor the Ephesians once had for the service to the Lord had somehow grown cold. Though the Lord didn't go into specifics, the fact is that it really didn't make a difference. The remedy is to go back and do the things that you did at first. This is why restarting is important. There is nothing new that you haven't already done at stake here; you just need to rekindle your fire.

When I say fire, what do I mean? Fire is a metaphor for fervor, drive, excitement and passion. As Jeremiah stated, God's Word was uncontainable because it was *like fire shut up in his bones*. A person being filled with God's Spirit was likened to fire when the Scriptures speak of being *baptized with fire*, and on the Day of Pentecost, those in the upper room experienced a miraculous phenomenon of *tongues of fire*. In each case, what follows *the fire* is power, passion, enthusiasm and excitement in the context of relationship. Whenever the fire has gone out, it means there is a lack of passion. Whenever the flames of passion are quenched, everything becomes dull and mundane, which leads to dissatisfaction. When people become dissatisfied, they often resort to blaming others for how they feel. They become critical and negative. Everything and everybody is wrong except for them.

All of this is symptomatic of the flames of passion going out. The loss of passion can affect an individual or an entire congregation. Such was the case with the church of Ephesus, to whom Jesus declared, "You have forsaken the love you had at first." Whenever you forsake the love for something or someone, the flame is soon to sputter out. Once the flame is out, there is no intensity. You have set your affections elsewhere and this becomes the problem. Your affections become divided, and you are split between loving Christ and another.

There is nothing like witnessing the enthusiasm of a newborn Christian. They love everything about serving God, no matter what they are asked to do. Wherever it is they have to serve, they are willing and ready. But when the newness wears off, their passion and intensity begin to burn out. Soon, the things they would readily do now take effort.

Losing your first love has consequences, such as affecting your service to the Lord. Remember what Jesus said, "I am the vine, you are the branches. Without me you can do nothing." When we lose our first love, it's like being disconnected from the vine. A lone branch can do nothing on its own. It is totally dependent upon the vine for everything, which is why disconnecting from the branches is so detrimental. Therefore, the fire going out is a "losing your first love" issue that will eventually hinder or destroy a relationship.

The remedy for this is the same today as it was for the believers at Ephesus: we have to do what we did at first to restart the fire. We must get rid of whatever has divided our attention that's keeping us from seeking the Lord. This is a fundamental principle that we see playing out in Genesis. After Adam and Eve sinned, they hid themselves from the Lord (Gen. 3:9). Sin and immorality cause us to recoil from the Lord. When we do that, we are no longer walking in the light. John's admonition on this subject is informative and effective:

> If we say we have fellowship with him while we walk in darkness, we lie and do not practice the truth. But if we walk in the light, as he is in the light, we have fellowship with one another, and the blood of Jesus his Son cleanses us from all sin.
>
> 1 John 1:6-7

This passage is simple, and requires no detailed exegesis. Three words in this passage are key: *light, fellowship* and *purify*. Having a close relationship with the Lord, where the fire is (the light), keeps us in fellowship (walking in the light), and burns off the sin (our daily falling short, not habitual sin that breaks fellowship), which purifies us through the continual washing of the blood of the Lamb. We must forsake sin and seek holiness, because without holiness no one will see the Lord. Even so, our daily living in a sinful world, among an unrighteous and wicked generation, means we cannot avoid getting dirty. Therefore, a benefit from walking closely with the Lord is being continually washed in His precious blood, which allows us to maintain fellowship.

STAY FOCUSED ON GOD AND THE ASSIGNMENT

Secondly, we need to stay focused on our assignment. What has God called you to do? One of the biggest impediments to having a fulfilling life of service to the Lord is when we are not living out our calling. Each Christian is given a gift and a measure of faith to use our gift to serve God and the people of God. Therefore, we must be intentional about walking in our purpose. Whenever we are out of purpose, we are off our assignment. The bottom line is that if you are not on purpose, you are off target, and you will always miss the mark that God has called you to.

With all of the things that are going on in the church and the world at large, it is very easy to get distracted, where we start focusing on the wrong things. How many times have you gone to check your email, but got distracted by clicking on some news, or product solicitation link put before your eyes on the way to your inbox? After clicking on one link after another, you finally get to your email, but you have wasted fifteen or twenty minutes of your time. This was by design. E-commerce experts get your attention by distracting with information that interests you. They monitor your online activity and searches to develop a profile of your interests, and through high-tech algorithms they send commercial information your way that is tailored just for you. The hope is to hook you through displaying what interests you to trigger impulse buying, transferring your money to their pockets. It's all a setup to get you every time.

This is a good example of how easy it is to become distracted. Satan attempted a similar technique with Jesus, when he took the Lord to a high mountain and showed the Lord all the kingdoms of the earth and their splendor and glory, and then offered them to Him. The only thing Jesus had to do was bow and worship the devil. Satan assumed if he let the Lord see the glamor of wealth, riches and materialism that he would distract Jesus from His ultimate purpose, which was going to the cross. Not a chance!

UNDERSTANDING HAPPINESS

You must understand happiness. You must understand what motivates you. You must understand why you are about to make your next move in ministry. Is it about pride, position or purpose? There are so many pastors, preachers, and clergy people, who are considering leaving where they are currently serving because they are not "happy." So now, the compass that inspires their direction is their sense of "happiness," not the Lord's leading. I'm not happy, so let me go somewhere where I can find happiness. But let me tell you now, you are responding to the wrong emotion, and you could make an impulsive move that could ruin your ministry and desire to serve God. The proverbial saying is true. "The grass is always greener on the other side."

Why were you created? That question requires an answer. Was it so you can experience happiness? I think not. You were created with a specific purpose in mind. Therefore, you should develop a life purpose statement that speaks to why God created you and what it is that you are to do in life. Regularly ask yourself, are you living your purpose? Purpose will keep you during times of uncertainty and strain. Be careful not to follow provisions instead of purpose. When purpose drives you, peace will ultimately show up at your front doorstep. Purpose is the only thing that can give us complete satisfaction in life. "With all thy knowing, know thy purpose."

For example, David became very upset when the Philistines refused to let him fight with them against their common enemy, King Saul. David would have been happy to finally get some payback against King Saul, who had been running him down for ten years. However, that would have been a bad move, because little did David know, God would appoint him king over Israel shortly after that battle. That was God's purpose for David. Sometimes, we just have to stick it out where we are serving and let patience have its perfect work, and not give in to what we think will make us happy.

Yes, there will be times you experience unhappiness. Jesus' life was full of unhappiness because He was surrounded by people who hated Him, lied about Him, didn't believe in Him and eventually crucified Him. Even the Lord asked the Father if there was any other way. He could come to no other conclusion and relented, saying, "Not my will, but thy will be done." The Garden of Gethsemane was not about reaching a place of happiness, but it was where the Lord came face to face with the weight and awesomeness of His purpose. Therefore, you cannot always self-regulate based upon your feeling of happiness, because what makes you happy today could cause you grief tomorrow. Unfortunately, many pastors have walked away from their calling based upon not being happy. If they would have stuck it out, they would have reached the fulfillment that God had planned for them.

Pride, Position or Purpose

There was a time when I was working at Trinity Evangelical Divinity School at an extension location at a church where the pastor was also a dean at Trinity and a very dear friend, Dr. Mike Reynolds. The extension school position didn't pay much money, while my bills were adding up. While working at this extension site, another job opened up. I informed Dr. Reynolds that I was considering leaving Trinity and the small church in Chicago where I was pastoring, and taking a staff job at another prominent church that was offering a six-digit salary. Well, the money and prestige were irresistible. I saw this as a blessing from the Lord and an answer to prayer, because my financial situation was tenuous.

However, Dr. Reynolds asked me a question that has stuck with me down through the years, which was, "Is this move about possessions or purpose?" That statement stumped me, but it didn't stop me. I went on to take that position, but it wasn't because of purpose, it was because of position and pride. Whenever pride and/or position are the primary motivations, you could end up making serious mistakes that could impact your ministry, marriage and your money. Whenever you step out from the Lord's will for your life, it's never about purpose, but you have succumbed to the intoxicating influence of position and pride.

When I made that move, it was about pride, because I was feeling like a failure because I was pastoring a small church I had started a few years earlier. I also made that move based upon provision because I needed the money. Examine yourself and seek wise counsel. Be careful about what is influencing your decision to move, understanding that in some cases it actually is time to move on. However, don't be so quick to move for the wrong reasons. There was a popular expression we used to say back in the day, "Check yourself, before you wreck yourself."

However, let's be clear, there is much happiness and fulfillment when you are walking in your purpose. In your purpose is where all of your power, provision and blessings are found. Therefore, purpose and happiness are not necessarily mutually exclusive; they are often conjoint. However, you cannot be merely driven by the *pursuit of happiness*, this will make you too vulnerable to distractions and deception, and will cause you to be easily pulled off course.

MOVING TO A NEW ASSIGNMENT

Leaving from one church to another has to be done decently and in order. There are so many horror stories where ministers have left churches after scandal, embezzlement or some serious moral lapse. In some cases, they steal members, enticing many to follow them to start a "better ministry" that usually comes to nothing soon afterwards. However, you should leave a church in such a good manner where you are proud to use the former church as a reference. At some churches, even when lay persons leave, they leave with a letter of good standing and go with the pastor's blessing. Leaving after a fallout is never the best way. If at all possible, leave on good terms.

Before leaving a church, ask the following questions:

(1) Is it because of pride, position, or purpose?

(2) Are you leaving knowing that you are going to the right place? Not every place is right for you. We all have our personalities and idiosyncrasies, and so do churches. As I have covered in previous chapters, you must assure you are serving in the right place.

(3) Have you done your due diligence and checked out where you are going?

(4) Have you gotten before the Lord in prayer to ascertain whether this is the will of God or just an impulse move you are contemplating?

(5) Have you prepared the people for it? If you are pastoring, you cannot wait until the week before you are leaving to tell everyone that you are transitioning. If you do that, you will damage and hurt a lot of souls. Leaving can be an emotional experience for which people must be prepared.

If you have covered these bases, your transition will be a lot smoother, and the grace of God will follow you to your next assignment.

All these issues I have covered in this chapter are related because they address how you must govern yourself in the ministry. You keep your fire burning by staying in close relationship with the Lord. You must maintain your effectiveness in ministry by staying focused on your assignment and not becoming distracted. You also should have a good understanding of what makes you happy, but also realize that you cannot afford to be mislead by the pursuit of happiness.

As you move forward in ministry, you must have a good understanding of what is motivating your decisions on where to serve: is it pride, position or purpose? And finally, how to move to your next assignment. Do you understand that how you leave where you are currently serving can determine the success you will have at your next assignment? You must live right, serve right and leave right so that God can bless your next steps and you can accomplish all that God has called you to do.

CHAPTER 22

NURSING OLD WOUNDS

Brothers, I do not consider that I have made it my own.
But one thing I do: forgetting what lies behind and strain-
ing forward to what lies ahead, I press on toward
the goal for the prize of the upward
call of God in Christ Jesus.
Philippians 3:13-14

In chapter 19, I covered the topic of how to navigate through a church fight. As I discussed, these fights can be very disruptive and quite traumatic. There are many stories of pastors being locked out of their church, kicked out of their parsonages, sued in court, arrested, physically attacked, and even facing false accusations ranging from adultery to pedophilia. As a result of going through a brutal church fight, some pastors have ended up in divorce, had to seek counseling, have experienced financial ruin, left the church altogether, turned to substance abuse, and some have become depressed and committed suicide.

It is expected that when someone is in a serious fight, there will be some physical wounds like cuts, bruises, abrasions and even broken bones. In time, these injuries usually heal but often leave a scar. However, long after the physical wounds have healed, emotional wounds can linger and cause secondary problems stemming from a fight long ago. Depending upon how pronounced these emotional wounds and trauma are, a person can suffer from a clinical condition called Post

Traumatic Stress Disorder (PTSD). PTSD is where the individual frequently relives the traumatic event, causing a number of psychological issues that impede a person's daily functioning and ability to cope with the typical stressors of life. Sights, sounds, persons, places and things can trigger a reaction that causes a person to relive that traumatic event. In other words, they cannot get past it.

Why Do People Nurse Old Wounds?

Most of us are fairly resilient, meaning we can handle our share of stress and disappointment, and bounce back without any major issues. But we are not all the same. Some people recover well from a traumatic event, others do not. But one way or another, we are all affected by trauma. The level and emotional depth the trauma has penetrated could determine how well one recovers from being hurt.

In chapter 20, I discussed the reality that a pastor is not a machine. We are impacted by the same range of emotions and feelings as anyone else in our congregations. We are not invulnerable to having our feelings hurt, being insulted, antagonized or becoming frustrated. Like David said, "Oh, that I had the wings of a dove! I would fly away and be at rest" Psalm 55:6, NIV. Being in leadership has its highs and lows. With all of the occupational hazards I've already covered, there is still an expectation that we will lead God's people with integrity and honesty as God gives us the strength and wisdom to do so. Not only are we accountable to men, but also to God.

Understanding all of the aforementioned, it is not unreasonable that sometimes pastors end up nursing old wounds. Though there may be some deeply hurtful circumstances that may have precipitated the bitterness that can follow being hurt, the main reason for nursing old wounds is simple. They haven't gotten over it.

Steps to Recovery

In order to get over an emotional wound, you first must acknowledge that someone has deeply hurt you. This isn't always easy, because it involves moving self out of the way and admitting this issue really bothered you. It got next to you. Many times we don't want to give others the satisfaction of knowing that they hit a soft spot. We don't like feeling vulnerable or admitting it. But if you are going to get past the pain, you have to be real about it and confess it. Do not cover this up. Remember that you are not a machine. The hurt emotions over this issue must be released, or they will become a root of bitterness. That root will take on a life of its own and destroy your ministry. Take this issue to the Lord in prayer, get counseling, find a trusted person with whom you can share your burdens.

The next step is to forgive. Forgiving people who hurt you is a difficult thing to do, but it must be done. First of all, unforgiveness is a sin, and it opens the door for Satan to take advantage of us (2 Cor.2:10-11). And the Scriptures are clear, if you do not forgive men of their trespasses, God will not forgive you of yours. We all need to have forgiving hearts. We forgive people not for the sake of people who harmed you, but for your own sake, and your mental and spiritual stability. Lastly, you must forgive others to maintain your relationship with God.

After you have forgiven, turn this issue over to God, and move on. The only way to get out of a bad place is to move on to a different place. Move on to another assignment. Do not stay stuck in the past. Do not keep checking the rear-view mirror. Do not keep turning back, move on. This is what Paul teaches in Philippians when he says, "…But one thing I do: Forgetting what is behind and straining toward what is ahead, I press on toward the goal to win the prize for which God has called me heavenward in Christ Jesus." No man can change the past, and God does not rewrite history. So you can either stay stuck, or press on to get that prize.

What Happens If…

So, what happens if you do not go through the steps to heal from church hurt? You take all the hurt, pain and bitterness on to the next church, and you will try to make them pay for a debt they do not owe. In effect, you will be nursing old wounds at a new church.

How many times have we counseled with married couples who were dealing in their current marriage with residual hurt from a previous marriage? One spouse struggles with trust, because in a past marriage there was infidelity. Now in the new marriage, the hurt spouse is needlessly suspicious and smothering because they cannot get over how the previous spouse hurt them. So the hurt from the old marriage dictates the terms of the new marriage, which is ruining any chance of the new marriage surviving.

The marriage situation cited here is similar to a pastor who has come through a church fight without resolving the hurt suffered at the former church. If a pastor moves on physically, but not emotionally, he is only bringing the old wounds to a new congregation that had nothing to do with the circumstances of the past. Therefore, instead of giving himself a fighting chance at the new church, he has shot himself in the foot, but blaming the new congregation for the wound. Now they are the ones who have to pay for the mistakes that the other congregation made. Effectively, the new pastor is sabotaging his new assignment because of old wounds he intends on nursing at his next assignment.

How do you know if you have moved on and healed from your old wounds? Ask yourself, *How do I actually feel about the people who hurt me?* If you cannot answer that question, then you need to fix the wound before you injure innocent people by spreading symptoms of your old wounds.

This is why you must acknowledge that you were wounded, forgive those who hurt you, turn it over to God, don't look back, and move on. You are not a machine. You are a human being. Unresolved church hurt will resurface and destroy new relationships.

Years ago, when I was pastoring a church on the South Side of Chicago, I was so frustrated with having to deal with power-hungry deacons that when I was working on my doctoral dissertation, I set out to prove that elder leadership in the church was a better system. I soon realized that I was nursing an old wound, and it was showing up in my dissertation. I was setting out to prove something that was not necessarily true, based upon what happened to me at a previous church. We must be careful not to carry bad baggage from our past to our future.

GROWING IN GRACE IN A NEW PLACE

God has designed and prepared you for such a time as this. Since it's new, take advantage of it. In a new place you have time and room to grow. Use the time to survey the layout and see the new possibilities. Plan anew and give yourself the chance to grow in grace there. It's okay to let yourself evolve. It's okay to test new approaches that are better suited for where you are currently serving. Along with the new challenges, there will also be opportunities to expand your knowledge base.

Remember, your steps have been ordered by the Lord. He is the One who is leading and guiding you. You are His tool that he uses to shape people into the image of Christ. That's why you learn from the past, but you do not let your past control or define your future. You are God's instrument, His under-shepherd. He uses you to perfect holiness in the lives of the people. At the new place you get to see God do new things and open up new doors that will take you to the next level in church leadership.

Understand your purpose. Understand who you are in Christ Jesus. Know the hope of your calling. Be courageous and be diligent. Understand the point of it all is to finish the race, to fight the good fight. Take encouragement from Paul's inspirational words to the Corinthian church:

"But thanks *be* to God, who gives us the victory through our Lord Jesus Christ. Therefore, my beloved brethren, be steadfast, immovable, always abounding in the work of the Lord, knowing that your labor is not in vain in the Lord" (1 Corinthians 15:57-58, NKJV). Serve God well so that you will hear the Lord say to you, "Well done, my good and faithful servant. You have been faithful over a few things, I will make you ruler over many."

CHAPTER 23

THE POINT OF IT ALL

I have covered a lot of ground in this book, tackling some of the most important issues a minister can face in church leadership. Some of you reading this book are at a crossroad. You are not sure which way to go. You're not sure if you want to be in a pastor's role in a local church, or whether you can serve the Lord in some other capacity in church leadership. Many of you have already started pastoring. In that case, hopefully you have walked away with some of my priceless jewels that you can incorporate into your ministry and life.

Others reading this book are at the beginning point of their ministry, having just completed seminary, and are heading for their first assignment as a pastor. Hopefully you haven't been dissuaded by some of the examples I use in this book. As you have discovered, there is a lot your seminary curriculum did not cover. Hopefully, you will have a more realistic as opposed to an idealistic approach to executing church leadership. Still others are in between what to do and where to go, and haven't made a decision as to which career path in ministry to take. The truth is that there is a lot more to do in ministry other than being a pastor.

For those of you who have chosen to accept that first pastoral assignment, I want you to understand that whereas being a pastor is a job, it's not just a job. I implore you: please do not enter the ministry simply because you have the educational credential that legitimizes your academic qualifications. Pastoring is not like going to school to be a dentist. Pastoring is different, because it has an academic side and a spiritual side that requires that the individual have a relationship with God.

Unfortunately, there are those who pastor who do not believe the Bible or that Christ rose from the dead, who do not have a redeeming relationship with God. To them, it's simply a career assignment where they have benefits and draw a paycheck. Indeed, they wear the title *pastor*, but they have not been called by God. Again, I say, pastoring is a job, but it's not just a job. It requires that a person be called by God, and be gifted specifically to lead God's people. Your academic degree alone cannot help you with this requirement.

Since pastoring is a ministry gift that requires a calling, that means there is a point to it, a reason for it, a divine prerogative that must be worked out in time and eternity by Him that brings to pass all things according to the divine counsel of His own will. In other words, behind everything that God does, there is a purpose. Therein, is the point of it all.

In 1 Peter 5, the apostle gives a timeless exhortation to those called into the ministry to lead God's people:

> So I exhort the elders among you, as a fellow elder and a witness of the sufferings of Christ, as well as a partaker in the glory that is going to be revealed: shepherd the flock of God that is among you, exercising oversight, not under compulsion, but willingly, as God would have you; not for shameful gain, but eagerly; not domineering over those in your charge, but being examples to the flock. And when the chief Shepherd appears, you will receive the unfading crown of glory. Likewise, you who are younger, be subject to the elders. Clothe yourselves, all of you, with humility toward one another, for "God opposes the proud but gives grace to the humble."
>
> 1 Peter 5:1-5

In this great exhortation there are several noteworthy aspects to ponder that time will simply not allow here. Therefore, I choose to focus on verses 2 and 3, because in these verses there is a divine imperative concerning righteous service and pastoral conduct, respect for God's people, and the expectation that your service as a pastor will be evaluated and rewarded in eternity. This is why you cannot walk into this vocation with a cavalier attitude. Pastoring is serious. People's souls are at stake, and you will give an account to God concerning how you shepherded His flock. Therefore, you must understand and embrace the point of it all.

"Shepherd the flock of God that is among you, exercising oversight, not under compulsion, but willingly, as God would have you." The idea here is that a pastor be a compassionate leader who is ultimately more concerned about the welfare of the sheep. Not in some compulsory, perfunctory manner having no real connection with the flock. Instead, allowing the love of God to work through him to feed and stand spiritual guard over their souls, as Jesus, the Good Shepherd did when he laid his life down for us all.

"Not for shameful gain, but eagerly; not domineering over those in your charge, but being examples to the flock." Shameful gain refers to those who are opportunists, who enter the ministry for the position, pride and prestige. Yes, you can get rich in the ministry. Yes, you can make a name for yourself. Yes, you can have a lot of prestige and power, but if this is the agenda you bring to the ministry, get out before you get hurt and damage the souls of them who entrusted their spiritual wellbeing to your care.

Another area of concern is that some people, once they are in a leadership role, feel that they must become a tyrant in order to force people's loyalty and compliance. This should not be. God is in control. These are not your people, and this is not your church. Whenever you assume a possessive role, you are no longer operating in and through the love of God, and your ego regulates how you manage and lead God's people. You are not called to be a dictator. You are called to be a servant. In order to be a servant, a spirit of humility must rest upon you so that you remember that you too were just as lost as anyone else except for the grace of God that saved and redeemed you.

Therefore, you are to be an example to the flock. You are to live righteously, and not be a hypocrite. If you preach the sermon, live the sermon. If you teach the Bible, obey the Bible. Everyone in the congregation watches your every move. Whereas none of us are perfect and you will make your share of mistakes, you are supposed to be the beacon and example of what it is to live a vicarious life in Christ. This is why God says in this text that you are an example, you are on display as God's workmanship, a pastor in which God is well pleased.

"And when the chief Shepherd appears, you will receive the unfading crown of glory." Whenever you are serving in the ministry, make sure that everything that you do is "as unto the Lord," which means always offer God and the people of God your best. In this you will understand the point of it all. Make no mistake about it, a divine payday is coming. Therefore, pastoring is not an exercise in futility, but a divine vocation that carries an eternal weight of glory. What you do on earth for the Lord as a pastor these relatively few years will impact you in glory, forever.

The point of it all is to consecrate God before the people, not ourselves. Pastors must always be an example of what it is to be a Christian in the true sense of the word. The point of it all is that no matter what gifts or talents we have, no matter what degree we have earned, no matter what status or resources God has allowed us to have, we must realize that it all came from Him in the first place. We are merely giving back through service what God has already given to us.

The point of it all is to love God with all our heart, mind and soul, and give Him the glory in all that we do. In the closing words of the book of Ecclesiastes, Solomon "the preacher," the wisest man who ever lived, sums it up this way:

> The words of the wise are like goads, and like nails firmly fixed are the collected sayings; they are given by one Shepherd. My son, beware of anything beyond these. Of making many books there is no end, and much study is a weariness of the flesh. The end of the matter; all has been heard. Fear God and keep his com-

mandments, for this is the whole duty of man. For God will bring every deed into judgment, with every secret thing, whether good or evil.

Ecclesiastes 12:11-14

It cannot be said any better than how King Solomon has said it here. This is the conclusion and indeed, the point of it all.

CHAPTER 24

PASTORING THROUGH A PANDEMIC

Some twenty-six hundred years ago, Habakkuk gave a prophecy that finds critical application to Christians and the world at large here in the 21st century. Habakkuk writes "Look at the nations and watch—and be utterly amazed. For I am going to do something in your days that you would not believe, even if you were told (Habakkuk 1:5, NIV). Historically, Habakkuk prophesied about the invasion of the Babylonians. However, this prophecy is fitting for what has transpired globally in 2020. If someone would have told me about the circumstances that would neutralize the nations and close down churches, like the prophet said, I would not have believed them.

We brought in 2020 on a very positive note. New Year's eve night are always special. Each year we conduct our traditional high-spirited watch night services where we give thanks for the old year and pray in the new year with great expectation. Two power-packed services. Standing room only. We prayed, we preached, and we praised. And with renewed vigor, we embraced our vision and affirmed our motto "Winning the world for Jesus." When the clock struck 12 a.m., the doors of promise and purpose swung open to great expectation for a fulfilling and fruitful new year. However, little did anyone know the cliff we were heading towards. We would be introduced to an ominous new term, COVID-19.

None of us were prepared to be redefined by this completely unforeseen pestilence. Once people started dying by the tens of thousands, life as we knew it changed forever. No sector of society went unscathed. Social distancing went into effect. Governors outlawed or greatly regulated, social gatherings, which devastated schools, businesses large and small, sports events and especially church assemblies. Now every church and every pastor were forced to adjust to the reality left in the wake of the Coronavirus.

It is safe to say, that no one in our lifetime has ever pastored through a pandemic. What this essentially means is that we are all in uncharted waters. There was no playbook, no template, no seven easy steps, that would help guide us through. We were all caught flatfooted. I'm wondering, where were all those so-called prophets and prognosticators then? No one saw this coming. Not only had anyone ever anticipated a pandemic of such magnitude, no one expected that it would last so long.

Initially, the church was faced with questions of how we could continue doing church when we could not physically meet? I remember receiving calls from pastors acknowledging the fact that we are in the midst of a pandemic, but still having the spiritual mandate to continue doing church.

MAINTAIN THE CONNECTION

One of the first challenges pastors faced was how to keep people connected. This is important because no matter what the circumstance that prevents gathering together as a congregation, connection still must be maintained. However, in maintaining that connection, some level of normalcy must be maintained. Immediately we started to adapt. Some pastors came up with the idea of a skeleton crew of staff conducting service as normal, but preaching to an empty room. Certainly, this was a dynamic that most pastors were not quite accustom to because preaching is a reactionary art. The preacher's sermon evokes congregational responses that causes a powerful spirit of exhortation throughout the church. This is an important dynamic. But when you are preaching to an empty room, it's all about delivering good content, without the payoff of the intermittent "amen" or "Hallelujah" from the pews.

On the other hand, how would the congregants sitting at home respond to service conducted virtually? Could pastors keep congregants engaged on a mobile device or at home with all distractions, typically found in the home? Pastors were also concerned if people would continue to support the ministry financially when they are not in actual attendance? All of these circumstances forced adaptations without any historical experience to draw from.

Initially, there was optimism in all of this. After we passed the acceptance stage of being in a pandemic, pastors were hopeful that this too would "soon" pass. But that wasn't the case. The pandemic lingered, month after grueling month. So, Pastors had to keep adjusting and were forced to learn by doing. This called for taking unusual steps to keep up with unprecedented times. Therefore, the Coronavirus conundrum presented several learning and growing opportunities we would have never considered under the norms of the past. COVID-19 quickly became a make-or-break proposition, without a playbook to consult. It was vitally important that if pastors and churches were going to make it, we had to give ourselves to prayer for God's guidance on what to do. Those churches, that continued to be successful, were clearly due to God's direction and not mere human ingenuity.

The H1N1 influenza pandemic of 1918 killed 650,000 in America and a global death toll of 50 million. During that time people did not have the knowledge nor the access to technology that we have today. Now God has blessed this generation with several modalities to communicate and stay connected. Whereas many ministries already had websites and presence on various social media platforms, no one could have imagined that churches would be relegated to conduct their worship services on Facebook, Facetime, Zoom and other platforms. What this has taught pastors is that churches should stay abreast of emerging technologies that can be incorporated into their worship experience. The big advantage to utilizing these technologies is it allows people to still gather, without the requirement to come together physically, thus greatly expanding the paradigm of congregation and community.

Though some found an upside to distance and virtual worship, still others saw a conflict between the biblical mandates and the state requirement to adhere to mitigation protocols that directly impacted church attendance. Some pastors were in arms, citing the violation of their constitutional rights, while others chose to adapt. Attempting to fuse together opposing realities of having church, while staying out of church, and complying with God's mandate to assemble ourselves together can put you in the wilderness of indecisiveness, the place where imprudent decisions are made. On the other hand, ignoring governmental mandates puts you in the crosshairs of state and local law enforcement. This presented a thin tightrope for pastors to balance several weighty factors, while attempting to do what is best for the congregation. As we have seen, some church services became the super-spreader events that have taken the lives of pastor and members alike.

For all of the various reasons stated, pastoring during a pandemic has been the most challenging context for pastoral leadership. It is similar to those nations where the church must remain underground, due to open persecution of those that follow Jesus. Historically this has always been the case. Even from the very beginning, the church has had to survive and even thrive under very extreme conditions. The main reason is what Jesus stated in Matthew's gospel, "I will build my Church and the gates of hell shall not prevail against it." The church is going to be alright, but how we do church in adverse conditions is going to require pastors to church outside of the box. This means we must understand what the components of church is all about.

THE COMPONENTS

In regards to the components of church, while in prayer, the word connected resonated in my spirit. What that entailed was that I was to do everything that I could to keep the church connected. Whether it is a pandemic or not, the church staying connected is important in any context. Connection is fundamental to the church because we are members of one body whether its locally or universally. It is imperative that we utilize any available technology to keep the church connected. Even though people were under "stay at home orders" isolated for a lengthy period of time, it was my job to do everything possible to keep them connected. Our members staying connected was not just for church, but for the support that people need during a health crisis that morphed into social and economic calamity. The last thing that people need is to feel that they are in a crisis alone. Therefore, church must learn how to adapt in order to stay purposeful and effective.

A good friend of mine, Dr. Freddie Haynes once said, "Even churches must learn to recreate or they will evaporate." What this means is that churches must utilize everything that they have to adapt to this new normal or become ineffective or obsolete. COVID-19 has caused us to rethink how we do church. We must anticipate that there will be future circumstances that will come to test the stamina and stability of our local congregations. Recreate or evaporate applies to any church no matter what size or socioeconomic status, ethnic composition, or geographical location. Every church must be prepared and execute "upping your game" in order to stay effective and connected.

In the midst of any circumstance that causes people to rethink and adapt, it is inevitable that people will choose different paths to reach their desired goal. Denominational churches typically have governing bodies that can disseminate information and give directions. However, many churches are independent, and pastors have to make decisions to the best of their ability. Some pastors saw staying connected differently than others. Some churches had already integrated doing church with technology. Still others were not, and mandates not to meet, did not sit well with many pastors. Some pastors complied, while others defied stay at home orders, and held church services regardless of the risk. Those who decided to have church anyway were ridiculed by other pastors. Therefore, unnecessary finger pointing ensued. It was almost as if some had forgotten who was the real enemy.

It is important to understand, that each church is a unique organism, each having its own context. We should never judge another pastor for how he reacts to what God has called him to do. The reason I say this is because I believe that this pandemic was a "God moment." God and only God could stop us simultaneously, across the globe. He made everyone stay home, made us pay attention to what we were doing, and made us evaluate how we did what we were doing.

What's Important?

Stress has a way of revealing weakness. During this pandemic, many churches discovered certain aspects of how they functioned in the past, was not as effective as they once thought. Churches discovered that they had a lot of fat in the operation of ministries. Some realized that they had fat in their worship. In assessing where the fat is, you must ask the question, What's really important? The people are. But it's not the quantity of members in the congregation, but it's the quality of members that makes all the difference in the world.

It was Thom Rainer who said twenty percent of the people that worshipped in your ministry prior to the pandemic, would not return to your church post pandemic. There are various reasons for this. One of the reasons people will not return is because they realize that they do not have to and are settled in not attending church. Secondly, residual fear will keep them concerned about getting sick. Lastly, and probably most plausible, is that they have adjusted to participating in worship remotely.

As it pertains to the quality of members, if twenty percent will fall off post pandemic then attention should focus onto those that will return. These members tend to be more settled in their walk with the Lord and are fully invested in their faith and the cause of Christ. These mature Christian can see through the challenges that the pandemic posed and are not deterred by the inconveniences imposed by temporary social distancing. Therefore, it is critically important to focus on developing disciples, as opposed to focusing in on people joining church. It is so easy to get caught up in doing church and fine tuning the mechanism of ministry, instead of spending time in the Word and prayer. Concentrate on developing solid disciples that have the fortitude to stand fast even when circumstances become adverse.

Another aspect of how to develop quality members is in the presentation of ministry and programming. Once we went virtual, we discovered a few things. One, people who would sit through a two-hour service in the church, would not stay engaged for two hours on a mobile device. So we realized that it was necessary to cut some fat from our worship services, and streamline our presentation. While being sure to maintain high standards in the presentation where it involved staging and lighting. It was important to improve our television production quality to enhance our worship experience. People have difficulty doing mediocre. So virtual content must be appealing to the eye in order to affect necessary engagement. People often scroll through platforms as Facebook, searching for attractive content. If what your ministry is broadcasting is not quality, people will scroll right on by your page or website. The quality of the presentation is most important, not the quantity.

Though members could not assemble themselves physically, we still saw amazing growth in their faith as we engaged through maintaining the connection. Prayer lines, conference calls, small groups, social media, all became lifelines to keep people connected. A member of a large church complained, "I was hoping that I would have at least received a phone call or an email from the church just to check to see if I was okay. That call or email never came." This church has a television program, a cutting-edge website, text-to-give, and a social media presence, but that personal connection, wasn't there.

What we can learn from this is, keeping people engaged does not only happen from one-way media content. Making content interactive is most important in times like these. Watching a television program is one-way. Having a Zoom class or prayer line is interactive and personal. Those ministries that were able to incorporate cutting edge technology to keep people engaged, and that personal touch, still benefited from the supposed restrictions that the pandemic imposed. There are new methodologies that were forged from disaster, because many of these things will stay in use in the post pandemic church.

THE NEW NORMAL

One of the takeaways from this pandemic experience is what churching will be like post-pandemic. Those who think that things will just snap back into place as they were before, are sadly mistaken. The church has evolved and doing church has evolved. Earlier on in this chapter I mentioned the fact that I believe that COVID-19 was a "God moment." Not to say God caused COVID-19, but that through this God is speaking. The churches being closed forced us all to do some serious introspection and evaluation of what is really important. Was God pleased with all our pursuits and priorities? No. Many churches and pastors had drifted far off course. We act as though we were equal partners with God in this global enterprise to win souls for the kingdom. However, in reality many of us were actually building our own kingdoms to make a name for ourselves. God's response, I don't need any of this. We were like ancient Israel saying, "the temple of the Lord, the temple of the Lord." Well, God had to show Israel what he thought about them and their temple when he sent the Babylonians to destroy it and take Israel captive. God reset Israel. The Coronavirus is our reset button. It was as if God shut everything down and said, now you figure out how to do it right.

COVID-19 forced us to be better at ministry and to be more sensitive to the move of the Spirit in reaching souls for God. So often we want God to back our agendas at the expense of sacrificing God's agenda. The Coronavirus was a wakeup call. No matter what happens, or what doors are closed, what pestilences or disasters befall this world, ministry must continue. People were in distress. They were sick. They were dying. They were experiencing economic collapse. They were starving. They were anxious and distressed. Even though the churches were closed, we still had to fulfill our great commission, and do our job. How do we continue to fulfill the mandate of Christ, to teach the Word, preach the Word, and continue to worship? How do we gather people in front of their mobile devices, so that the church can still offer Christ during a time of pandemic? COVID-19 will not be the last global challenge this world will face. But what we learned from this pandemic will greatly inform and prepare us for the next one.

No matter what this world faces, calamity does not excuse us to become inactive. One way or another, we have to adapt. The church will still have to do its job. As Solomon declared in Ecclesiastes, "...no one is discharged in time of war" (Eccl. 8:8, NIV). We must stay and fight, because people need hope, help and healing of the hurt. These are the things that anyone facing challenging times must always address. Though it might be another hundred years before a pandemic strikes again, rest assured there will be other calamities that challenge our ability to assemble. We will have to be ready to operate under the principles and power of our faith, utilizing everything available to stay connected, while maintaining balance and Christ centeredness.

CHAPTER 25

THE NECESSITY OF A SOCIAL GOSPEL

ON WHICH END OF THE ROPE ARE YOU?

There is a big debate over whether the "Social Gospel" is biblical or not. Those who oppose a Social Gospel use a number of passages and semantic arguments to back their position. However, there seems to be a charge from the opposition that misapplies the word "Gospel." Those who are in favor of preaching a social gospel message are not attempting to supplant the core message of the death, burial, and resurrection of Jesus Christ. No one is advocating moving away from the fundamentals. However, with the social gospel, pastors who have a voice in the community and humanitarian concerns use their voice and pulpits to decry the inequalities that we find in everyday life, particularly here in America.

In a perfect world, America the land of the free, there would be no social inequities, oppression, or institutionalized racism. Therefore, a Social Gospel would not be necessary. But in a nation where all these thing still persist, the disadvantaged and disenfranchised need those who will cry out on their behalf.

In recent months, names such as Brianna Taylor, George Floyd, Eric Garner, Tamir Rice, Philando Castile, Laquan McDonald, Walter Scott, and so many more all died at the hands of the police. Twelve-year-old Tamir Rice, just being a kid, was playing in a park with a toy gun. Police road up and within seconds, shot him dead. Brianna

Taylor, an innocent bystander was shot 8 times in her own home while police raided her home looking for a person that was already in police custody. Philando Castile was shot 6 times at point-blank range while seated in the front seat of his car reaching for his license. Laquan McDonald was shot 16 times as he walked away from police. Walter Scott was shot 6 times in the back, while he posed no threat, running from the police. What do these all have in common? Overkill, being black and being killed by white police. And of course who can forget the horrible video where a police officer killed George Floyd who was handcuffed and pinned to the ground. For over 9 minutes, with his full weight on Floyd's neck, the officer showed no mercy or compassion for the life of another human being. In fact while his knee was on Floyd's neck, the officer's hand was on his hip as if to say, I can do this all day, while Floyd, plead for his life, even calling on his deceased mother to help him.

On the other hand, 17-year-old Kyle Rittenhouse shoots 3 people, killing 2 and seriously injuring a third person. With a semiautomatic long rifle draped around his neck, left two dead people lying in the street, walked by the police, without being stopped, or even questioned. But a black kid with a cell phone in his hand, dies in a hail of bullets running away from the police, where the police aren't even charged, let alone convicted. Where is the justice in that?

Let's face it. If it had not been for courageous Black ministers who dared to take up social causes from the pulpits to the streets, African Americans would still not be able to vote. Neither would they be able to live in the community of their choice, attend a school that has decent education, or be able to work on a job above the level of menial servitude.

I Can't Breathe

I believe this argument for a social gospel is simple, but it depends on which end of the proverbial rope you are on, whether you're holding the rope or hanging from the rope. The one holding the rope has so many convenient options. He has the luxury of deciding whether things should change or not. He has the time to go home and sleep on it for a while or to contemplate and consider all the nuances of what change should really look like. He is in the position to do nothing if he so pleases. He has the backing of an oppressive system that perpetuates the status quo that benefits him and his children. He has the advantage to keep things just as they are.

However, the one hanging from the rope has a completely different set of circumstances. He's being deprived of air that should be available to everyone. He can't breathe. He is choking. Yes, there are other issues in life to consider, but this one is the immediate issue, the ability to breathe determines whether he will live or die. The oppressed has a different perspective than his oppressor, but the one thing they have in common is that rope.

Therefore, a social gospel is spoken in the language of the oppressed and marginalized. It is the good news based on the hope that one day they will be free to breathe. It is the message that encourages the hearers not to give up hope, because even Christ Himself was from an oppressed and marginalized people who also spent 400 years in slavery. Those holding the rope, don't think of the Son of God, as being a descendant of slaves, but he was. Those holding the rope fail to consider what Jesus declared would be a determining factor in judgment in His Kingdom,

> Then the King will say to those on his right, 'Come, you who are blessed by my Father, inherit the kingdom prepared for you from the foundation of the world. For I was hungry and you gave me food, I was thirsty and you gave me drink, I was a stranger and you welcomed me, I was naked and you clothed me, I was sick and you visited me, I was in prison and you came to me.' Then the righteous will answer him, saying, 'Lord, when did we see you hungry and feed you, or thirsty and give you drink? And when did we see you a stranger and welcome you, or naked and clothe you? And when did we see you sick or in prison and visit you?' And the King will answer them, 'Truly, I say to you, as you did it to one of the least of these my brothers, you did it to me.'   Matthew 25:34-40

One could make the argument that this passage is not speaking of preaching the Gospel. Or those who are Dispensational may claim this passage has nothing to do with the Church. However, the issue here is not so much who, but what. Pharisees have always focused on the law, the technicalities, the semantics, and are always judging the poor, oppressed, and the marginalized. So, it is with the Pharisees of today, they would rather argue doctrine, than to help people. You don't need to keep preaching the death, burial and resurrection to those who have already given their life to Christ. But after they come to Christ, teach them how to be proper representatives and ambassadors of God's kingdom.

If this nation was righteous and equal for all, you would not have all of the strife and division that is rife in society and the Church. Racism, prejudice, and oppression are still alive and well in the Church, and the election of 2016 and 2020 brought it boiling to the surface. Therefore, the oppressors should not think that after supporting a repressive system, that they have the moral authority to tell the oppressed what not to speak out against or whether a social gospel is biblical or not.

If you want to get rid of the social gospel, then eliminate what makes it necessary. Take the rope off my neck, and use it to pull me up to a status of equality. Those who keep silent on unrighteousness are complicit in the same. As pastors and preachers, we must be willing to take a stand. Noah's message was repent. Jonah's message to Nineveh was repent. John the Baptist's message was repent. The Apostles message on the day of Pentecost was repent. The Lord's message to Solomon for the people was,

> if my people who are called by my name humble themselves, and pray and seek my face and turn from their wicked ways, then I will hear from heaven and will forgive their sin and heal their land.   2 Chronicles 7:14

Why do you think the supposedly greatest nation on earth, has been stricken with the Coronavirus so extensively? Why have there been 50 mass shootings in America in the first four months of 2021? Why are the number of questionable police shootings still occurring nationwide? Why is racism, voter suppression, and inequality still the order of the day. Though America proudly displays the bald eagle as it's national symbol, it doesn't make a difference whether you are left wing or right wing, because they are both opposite wings of the same sick bird.

I'm afraid that God is speaking, but too few are listening. America is sick. Our land needs healing. Take the rope off my neck, so we can all be free to breathe the air of equality and glorify Christ together as one nation under God. As the apostle Paul so powerfully declares,

> For as many of you as were baptized into Christ have put on Christ. There is neither Jew nor Greek, there is neither slave nor free, there is no male and female, for you are all one in Christ Jesus.
>
> Galatians 3:27-28

Connect with the Author

For questions, comments, feedback, or engagement requests, Dr. Hughes would love to hear from you. Please send all inquiries to: djhughes45@gmail.com

ENDNOTES

1   https://www.seminarycomparison.com/enrollment/#

2   https://www.intrust.org/magazine/issues/spring-2014/ministers-without-masters-degrees

3   https://www.christianitytoday.com/history/people/evangelistsandapologists/dwight-l-moody.html

4   https://www.christianheadlines.com/contributors/milton-quintanilla/rzim-to-change-name-remove-content-related-to-zacharias.html

5   Matthew Henry's Commentary on the Whole Bible, Vol. 2, pg 675, *Sons of Issachar*

6   https://www.encyclopedia.com/education/news-wires-white-papers-and-books/youngblood-johnny-ray-1948

7   https://www.leadershipresources.org/blog/christian-ministry-burnout-prevention-signs-statistics-recovery/

About the Publisher

Let *Life to Legacy* bring your story to literary life! We offer the following publishing services: manuscript development, editing, transcription services, ghost-writing, cover design, copyright services, ISBN assignment, worldwide distribution, and eBook conversion.

We make the publishing process easy. Throughout production, we keep the author informed every step of the way. Even if you do not have a manuscript, that's not a problem for us. We can ghost-write your book from audio recordings or legible handwritten documents. Whether print-on-demand or trade publishing, we have packages to meet your publishing needs. At *Life to Legacy*, we take the stress out of becoming a published author.

Unlike other *so-called* publishers, we do more than just print books. Our books and eBooks are distributed to book buyers, distributors, and online retailers throughout the world. This is real publishing! Call us today for a free quote.

Please visit our website
www.Life2Legacy.com

or call us
877-267-7477

Send email inquiries to
Life2Legacybooks@att.net